JEFFERSON
AT MONTICELLO

JEFFERSON AT MONTICELLO

Memoirs of a Monticello Slave
as dictated to Charles Campbell by Isaac

Jefferson at Monticello:
The Private Life of Thomas Jefferson
by Rev. Hamilton Wilcox Pierson

Edited, with an Introduction, by

James A. Bear, Jr.

University Press of Virginia
Charlottesville

The University Press of Virginia

Tenth printing 1995

The frontispiece illustration
of Jefferson is the pencil sketch
by Benjamin Henry Latrobe
drawn from life about 1799.
(Courtesy of the Maryland Historical Society)
    This sketch also appears on
the cover of the paper edition together with
the west elevation of Monticello as drawn
by Robert Mills about 1803.
(Courtesy of the Massachusetts Historical Society)

ISBN: Cloth, 0-8139-0021-2;
paper, 0-8139-0022-0

Library of Congress
Catalog Card Number: 67–17629
Printed in the
United States of America

Editor's Note

CHARLES W. CAMPBELL'S handwritten manuscript of Isaac's recollections is now in the Tracy W. McGregor Library at the University of Virginia. Campbell recorded this narrative in 1847 in Petersburg, Virginia, where he found Isaac living in quiet retirement after his many years of service to Jefferson. The memoirs were not published at that time and, indeed, lay silent for more than a century until they were discovered and published in a scholarly edition under the editorship of Dr. Rayford W. Logan in 1951. Interest in this classic of domestic life at Monticello was immediate. In 1955 a second, popular edition was issued to meet the growing popularity of the work but it, like the first, has now gone out of print.

When Dr. Logan transcribed the manuscript, he sought to make the printed copy as much like the original as possible. Campbell's individual preferences in spelling, capitalization, and punctuation were preserved but at the cost of making the way rather difficult for modern readers more interested in the matter in the book than in its form. The popular edition regularized many of the eccentricities of spelling and capitalization but retained always the original touches which reflected directly Isaac's own pronunciation and his habits of speech. Campbell's comments, some footnotes, and genealogical charts of Isaac's family and the other large Monticello slave family, the Hemings, were placed at the end of the narrative. Nothing in the manuscript was omitted or suppressed, and information derived from other sources was clearly indicated.

The present text is based upon the earlier ones. It differs only in that it has been more carefully edited to conform with modern usage, the artificial chapter divisions have been dropped, the notes have been considerably enlarged and revised, and the genealogical charts have been reviewed. The parenthetical material introduced into the text by Charles Campbell has been retained.

Although taken down at a later date, the Rev. Hamilton W. Pierson's manuscript of recollections of life at Monticello by Jefferson's overseer, Edmund Bacon, has stubbornly resisted location. Pierson, who was president of Cumberland College in Princeton, Kentucky, gathered the material for his work during visits to Bacon's farm in nearby Trigg County. Fortunately this manuscript was published, probably very soon after it was completed, by Charles Scribner in 1862. It is virtually unknown today in spite of the liberal use James Parton made of it in his *Life of Jefferson* (1874). Parton's portrait caused a Jefferson grandson, Thomas Jefferson Randolph, to issue a critical rebuttal, "The Last Days of Jefferson," but whether or not Randolph had read Pierson's book is not known.

The text of the present edition is substantially that of the original. Letters, memorandums, and other quoted materials follow the printed text of Pierson's book except for the correction of a few obvious errors. The will has been checked and made to conform to the original. A closing chapter containing Pierson's sentiments for the Union in its hour of challenge has been omitted. His notes have been augmented by the present editor with the hope, as in the case of Isaac's *Memoirs*, that they may serve to place these documents in clearer historical perspective.

J. A. B., Jr.

Charlottesville, Virginia
October, 1966

Contents

Editor's Note   v

Introduction   xi

Memoirs of a Monticello Slave   1
    Genealogical Tables   facing p. 24

Jefferson at Monticello: The Private Life of
    Thomas Jefferson   25
    I   Introduction to Captain Bacon   27
    II   Bacon's Autobiography   39
    III   Monticello   46
    IV   Mr. Jefferson's Blooded Stock   58
    V   Mr. Jefferson's Manufactories   64
    VI   Mr. Jefferson's Personal Appearance and
           Habits   71
    VII   Mr. Jefferson's Family   83
    VIII   Mr. Jefferson's Servants   97
    IX   Mr. Jefferson at Washington – His
           Library   104
    X   Mr. Jefferson's Hospitality   111
    Appendix: Mr. Jefferson's Will   118
Notes   123

Index   138

Illustrations

Benjamin Latrobe's drawing
 of Thomas Jefferson   frontispiece

                                             facing

1. Isaac Jefferson in the 1840's   18

2. Jefferson's sketch of the west front of Monticello, ca. 1770   50

3. The west front of Monticello in the 1830's   51

Introduction

THE EVENTS of Thomas Jefferson's public life and the influence of his politics and philosophy have received a full measure of attention from generations of historians. Most of the biographies of our third President have been organized around the extraordinary happenings of his career because of their central importance to our national heritage. It seemed sometimes as if there was little room left for Jefferson "himself," his hopes and fears or his concerns and enthusiasms. Actually, little has been written about his domestic life—as little in proportion as the great deal about his public life.

Thomas Jefferson was a very reserved individual who believed that his private life was his own. Thus few persons knew him or his ways well enough, or were granted the opportunity of observing him long enough, to enable them to chronicle these private concerns. Two such persons, however, were Isaac, the slave, and Edmund Bacon, an overseer.

Their accounts reprinted in this book are the only substantial contemporary documents treating this fascinating and unexplored side of the master of Monticello. One cannot entirely discount Henry S. Randall's *Life of Jefferson* (1857), whose three large volumes contain in various places bits and pieces of contemporary information on this aspect of Jefferson's life, or *The Domestic Life of Jefferson* (1871), by a great-granddaughter, Sarah Nicholas Randolph, who treats her illustrious forebear chiefly as an amiable and kindly parent, grandparent, and master at

Monticello. Neither Randall nor Miss Randolph knew Jefferson, and their information was drawn from his writings and from recollections of his children, grandchildren, and close friends.

Bacon's and Isaac's narratives are unique in that each writer knew his subject from very close range. Their stories overlap in detail so that we can oppose and judge the information they provide. They emerge so much in agreement in what they say that we feel historical truth behind their informality. They complement each other in a different, more fortunate way. Isaac's recollections go back to the first days of life at Monticello, and Bacon's begin later to furnish more detail during the years when the old slave as he grew older became increasingly less involved in plantation affairs.

In both accounts "Mr. Jefferson" is the central figure. Isaac and Bacon, who represent the extremes of the Monticello service hierarchy, were each sixty-five years old when their recollections were taken down. What they remember best, of course, are scenes from the past made vivid and immediate by details involving their own experience. In these scenes Jefferson as the dominating figure always appears at a slight remove from the focus of memory. Probably this is neither a result of age nor a failure of skill in reporting, but truly represents Jefferson as he was and captures the natural reserve so many felt in his presence. Apparent at once in both accounts is a touching concern for the master whose involvement in national affairs made his life so different from their own. His other cares seemed to them to frustrate his enjoyment of the ordinary pleasures of the house and field, which were, after all, the objects of their concern.

Isaac's attitude during the forty-odd years he records

(from 1781 to 1824) is marked by his simple acceptance of persons and events. His recollections are not affected by harsh treatment any more than by indulgence granted a favorite. Isaac seems to have erred seriously in only a few instances, if one overlooks such references as those to General Riedesel as "Ginral Redhazel" and Yorktown as "Little York." Three errors are his reporting that his mother, the slave Ursula, was Martha's wet nurse at the same time she was nursing him (there was too great an age differential for this to be true), that the British entered Richmond in 1781 by way of Manchester, and that Jefferson went to Philadelphia in 1790 to serve as President (he was Washington's Secretary of State). These inconsistencies are errors of association not of fancy. They do not affect the usefulness or authenticity of Isaac's memoir. Its simplicity is its hallmark of truth.

Bacon's recollections of the years from 1806 to 1822 are different from Isaac's in a number of ways. His place in the overseer's house allowed him to observe a much wider range of people and events. He was able to witness affairs in the big house, at the toll mill, and on the farm and to move from the meanest slave cabin to, on one occasion at least, the President's house itself. Perhaps it was the freedom of movement dictated by his responsibilities that led Bacon to assume more intimacy with Jefferson in his account than seems likely to us today. In chapters such as "Mr. Jefferson's Personal Appearance and Habits," "Mr. Jefferson's Family," and "Mr. Jefferson's Servants" there is more than mere reporting. Bacon's easy access to Jefferson's room, his lending of furniture for use at Monticello, and his control over the house do not ring true. Jefferson Randolph, a grandson, firmly dismissed such claims.

These matters do not detract from the historical value of

Bacon's account because, of course, the flaws in his book are errors in the facts about himself, not about Jefferson. If there is concern for Jefferson in Bacon's recollections, there is also more than a hint of patronage and certainly something of the mental processes of the spy. One notices Bacon noticing. The careful overseer has his eye on everything. He rarely misses the opportunity to judge the train of events and often he covertly challenges the wisdom of his employer. His sons are even set up as examples for the Randolph grandchildren to emulate, and Jefferson's high praise for his good works is not forgotten.

Yet, in the end, one feels these attitudes are shaped less by envy than by the limitations of the man. Bacon could not see Jefferson as a public servant who preserved his private life and the pleasures of his country estate at an almost incalculable expenditure of effort and energy. Instead, he saw him as a farmer who unwisely permitted himself to be distracted from what was his proper business, the direction of his estate. And it is here that we find what is most valuable in his recollections of Jefferson. For in spite of himself Bacon registers something about the workings of that most mysterious quality—human greatness. He saw without realizing it Jefferson's ability to be the mirror of his fellow man and yet to remain, at the same time, unique among all men.

MEMOIRS OF
A MONTICELLO SLAVE
as dictated to
Charles Campbell by Isaac

ISAAC JEFFERSON was born at Monticello. His mother was named Usler but nicknamed "Queen," because her husband was named George and commonly called "King George." She was pastry cook and washer-woman; stayed in the laundry. Isaac toted wood for her, made fire, and so on.[1] Mrs. Jefferson would come out there with a cookery book in her hand and read out of it to Isaac's mother how to make cakes, tarts, and so on.

Mrs. Jefferson was named Patsy Wayles, but when Mr. Jefferson married her she was the Widow Skelton, widow of Batter Skelton. Isaac was one year's child with Patsy Jefferson; she was suckled part of the time by Isaac's mother.[2] Patsy married Thomas Mann Randolph.[3] Mr. Jefferson bought Isaac's mother from Colonel William Fleming of Goochland. Isaac remem-bers John Nelson, an Englishman at work at Monti-cello; he was an inside worker, a finisher.[4] The black-smith was Billy Ore;[5] the carriage maker Davy Watson.[6] He worked also for Colonel Carter of Blen-heim, eight miles from Monticello. Monticello house was pulled down in part and built up again some six or seven times.[7] One time it was struck by lightning. It had a Franklin rod at one end.[8] Old Master used to say, "If it hadn't been for that Franklin the whole house would have gone." They was forty years at work upon that house before Mr. Jefferson stopped building.

Mr. Jefferson came down to Williamsburg in a phaeton made by Davy Watson. Billy Ore did the ironwork. That phaeton was sent to London and the springs &c. was gilded. This was when Mr. Jefferson was in Paris.[9] Isaac remembers coming down to Williamsburg in a wagon at the time Mr. Jefferson was Governor. He came down in the phaeton, his family with him in a coach and four. Bob Hemings drove the phaeton; Jim Hemings was a body servant; Martin Hemings the butler. These three were brothers; Mary Hemings and Sally, their sisters.[10] Jim and Bob bright mulattoes; Martin, darker. Jim and Martin rode on horseback. Bob went afterwards to live with old Dr. Strauss in Richmond and unfortunately had his hand shot off with a blunderbuss.[11] Mary Hemings rode in the wagon. Sally Hemings' mother Betty was a bright mulatto woman, and Sally mighty near white; she was the youngest child. Folks said that these Hemingses was old Mr. Wayles's children.[12] Sally was very handsome, long straight hair down her back. She was about eleven years old when Mr. Jefferson took her to France to wait on Miss Polly. She and Sally went out to France a year after Mr. Jefferson went.[13] Patsy went with him at first, but she carried no maid with her. Harriet, one of Sally's daughters, was very handsome. Sally had a son named Madison, who learned to be a great fiddler. He has been in Petersburg twice; was here when the balloon went up, the balloon that Beverley sent off.

Mr. Jefferson drove faster in the phaeton than the

wagon. When the wagon reached Williamsburg, Mr. Jefferson was living in the College. Isaac and the rest of the servants stayed in the Assembly house, a long wooden building. Lord Botetourt's picture was there.[14] The Assembly house had a gallery on top running round to the College. There was a well there then; none there now. Some white people was living in one end of the house. A man named Douglas was there; they called him "Parson Douglas."[15] Mr. Jefferson's room in the College was downstairs. A tailor named Giovanni, an Italian, lived there too—made clothes for Mr. Jefferson and his servants.[16] Mrs. Jefferson was there with Patsy and Polly. Mrs. Jefferson was small;[17] she drawed from old Madam Byrd several hundred people and then married a rich man.[18] Old Master had twelve quarters seated with black people, but mighty few come by him; he want rich himself—only his larnin'. Patsy Jefferson was tall like her father. Polly low like her mother and longways the handsomest, pretty lady jist like her mother; pity she died—poor thing! She married John W. Eppes—a handsome man but had a harelip.[19]

Jupiter and John drove Mr. Jefferson's coach and four; one of 'em rode postilion. They rode postilion in them days. Traveling in the phaeton Mr. Jefferson used oftentimes to take the reins himself and drive. Whenever he wanted to travel fast *he'd* drive; would drive powerful hard himself.[20] Jupiter and John wore caps and gilded bands. The names of the horses was Senegore, Gustavus, Otter, Remus, Romulus, and Caractacus, Mr. Jefferson's riding horse.

After one year the government was moved from Williamsburg to Richmond.[21] Mr. Jefferson moved there with his servants, among 'em Isaac. It was cold weather when they moved up. Mr. Jefferson lived in a wooden house near where the palace stands now.[22] Richmond was a small place then, not more than two brick houses in the town—all wooden houses what there was. At that time from where the Powhatan house now stands clear down to the Old Market was pretty much in pines. It was a wooden house shedded round like a barn on the hill, where the Assemblymen used to meet, near where the Capitol stands now. Old Mr. Wiley had a saddler shop in the same house.[23] Isaac knew Billy Wiley mighty well—a saddler by trade; he was doorkeeper at the Assembly. His wife was a baker and baked bread and ginger cakes. Isaac would go into the bake oven and make fire for [her]. She had a great big bake oven. Isaac used to go way into the oven; when he came out Billy Wiley would chuck wood in. She sometimes gave Isaac a loaf of bread or a cake. One time she went up to Monticello to see Mr. Jefferson. She saw Isaac there and gave him a ninepence and said, "This is the boy that made fires for me." Mr. Jefferson's family servants then at the palace were Bob Hemings, Martin, Jim, house servants; Jupiter and John, drivers; Mary Hemings and young Betty Hemings, seamstress and housewoman; Sukey, Jupiter's wife, the cook.

The day before the British came to Richmond Mr. Jefferson sent off his family in the carriage. Bob Hemings and Jim drove. When the British was expected, Old Master kept the spyglass and git up by the skylight window to the top of the palace looking towards Williamsburg.[24] Some other gentlemen went up with him, one of them old Mr. Marsdell;[25] he owned where the basin is now and the basin spring. Isaac used to fetch water from there up to the palace. The British reached Manchester about 1 o'clock. Isaac larnt to beat drum about this time. Bob Anderson, a white man, was a blacksmith. Mat Anderson was a black man and worked with Bob. Bob was a fifer; Mat was a drummer. Mat 'bout that time was sort a-makin' love to Mary Hemings. The soldiers at Richmond, in the camp at Bacon Quarter Branch, would come every two or three days to salute the Governor at the palace, marching about there drumming and fifing. Bob Anderson would go into the house to drink; Mat went into the kitchen to see Mary Hemings. He would take his drum with him into the kitchen and set it down there. Isaac would beat on it and Mat larnt him how to beat.

As soon as the British formed a line, three cannon was wheeled 'round all at once and fired three rounds. Till they fired, the Richmond people thought they was a company come from Petersburg to join them; some of 'em even hurrahed when they see them coming; but that moment they fired everybody knew it was the British. One of the cannon balls knocked off the top of a butcher's house; he was named Daly, not far from the Governor's house. The butcher's wife screamed out and holler'd and her children too and all. In ten minutes not a white man was to be seen in Richmond;

they ran hard as they could stave to the camp at Bacon Quarter Branch. There was a monstrous hollering and screaming of women and children. Isaac was out in the yard; his mother ran out and cotch him up by the hand and carried him into the kitchen hollering. Mary Hemings, she jerked up her daughter the same way. Isaac run out again in a minute and his mother too; she was so skeered, she didn't know whether to stay indoors or out. The British was dressed in red. Isaac saw them marching. The horsemen (Simcoe's cavalry[26]) was with them; they come arter the artillerymen. They formed in line and marched up to the palace with drums beating; it was an awful sight—seemed like the Day of Judgment was come. When they fired the cannon, Old Master called out to John to fetch his horse Caractacus from the stable and rode off.

Isaac never see his Old Master arter dat for six months. When the British come in, an officer rode up and asked, "Whar is the Governor?" Isaac's father (George) told him, "He's gone to the mountains." The officer said, "Whar is the keys of the house?" Isaac's father gave him the keys; Mr. Jefferson had left them with him. The officer said, "Whar is the silver?" Isaac's father told him, "It was all sent up to the mountains." The old man had put all the silver about the house in a bed tick and hid it under a bed in the kitchen and saved it too and got his freedom by it. But he continued to sarve Mr. Jefferson and had forty pounds from Old Master and his wife. Isaac's mother had seven dollars a month for lifetime for washing, ironing, and making pastry.[27] The British sarcht the house but didn't disturb none of the furniture; but they plundered the wine cellar, rolled the pipes out and stove 'em in, knockin' the heads out. The bottles they broke the necks off with their swords, drank some, threw the balance away. The wine cellar was full; Old Master had plenty of wine and rum, the best. Used to have Antigua rum, twelve years old. The British next went to the corncrib and took all the corn out, strewed it in a line along the street towards where the Washington tavern is now (1847)[28] and brought their horses and fed them on it; took the bridles off. The British said they didn't want anybody but the Governor; didn't want to hurt him, only wanted to put a pair of silver handcuffs on him; had brought them along with them on purpose. While they was plunderin' they took all of the meat out of the meat house, cut it up, laid it out in parcels; every man took his ration and put it in his knapsack. When Isaac's mother found they was gwine to car him away, she thought they was gwine to leave her. She was cryin' and hollerin' when one of the officers came on a horse and ordered us all to Hylton's. Then they marched off to Westham. Isaac heard the powder magazine when it blew up—like an earthquake. Next morning between eight and nine they marched to Tuckahoe, fifteen miles;[29] took a good many colored people from Old Tom Mann Randolph. He was called "Tuckahoe Tom." Isaac has often been to Tuckahoe—a low-built house but monstrous large.[30] From Tuckahoe the British went to Daniel Hylton's. They carred off thirty people from Tuckahoe and some from Hylton's. When they come back to Richmond, they took all Old Master's from his house. All of 'em had to walk except Daniel and Molly (children of Mary the pastry cook) and Isaac. He was then big enough to beat the drum, but couldn't raise it off the ground; would hold it tilted over to one side and beat on it that way.[31]

There was about a dozen wagons along. They (the British) pressed the common wagons—four horses to a wagon; some black drivers, some white; every wagon guarded by ten men marching alongside.

One of the officers give Isaac name Sambo, all the time feedin' him. Put a cocked hat on his head and a red coat on him and all laughed. Coat a monstrous great big thing; when Isaac was in it, couldn't see nothin' of it but the sleeves dangling down. He remembers crossing the river somewhere in a periauger (piragua). And so the British carred them down to Little York (Yorktown). They marched straight through town and camped jist below back of the battlefield. Mr. Jefferson's people there was Jupiter, Sukey the cook, Usley (Isaac's mother), George (Isaac's father), Mary the seamstress, and children Molly, Daniel, Joe, Wormley, and Isaac. The British treated them mighty well; give 'em plenty of fresh meat and wheat bread. It was very sickly at York; great many colored people died there, but none of Mr. Jefferson's folks.[32] Wallis (Cornwallis) had a cave dug and was hid in there. There was tremendous firing and smoke—seemed like heaven and earth was come together. Every time the great guns fire Isaac jump up off the ground. Heard the wounded men hollerin'. When the smoke blow off, you see the dead men laying on the ground. General Washington brought all Mr. Jefferson's folks and about twenty of Tuckahoe Tom's (Tom Mann Randolph's) back to Richmond with him and sent word to Mr. Jefferson to send down to Richmond for his servants. Old Master sent down two wagons right away, and all of 'em that was carred away went up back to Monticello. At that time Old Master and his family was at Poplar Forest, his place in Bedford. He stayed there after his arm was broke, when Caractacus threw him.[33] Old Master was mightily pleased to see his people come back safe and sound and to hear of the plate.

Mr. Jefferson was a tall, strait-bodied man as ever you see, right square-shouldered. Nary man in this town walked so straight as my Old Master. Neat a built man as ever was seen in Vaginny, I reckon, or any place – a straight-up man, long face, high nose.

Jefferson Randolph (Mr. Jefferson's grandson) nothing like him, except in height – tall, like him; not built like him. Old Master was a straight-up man; Jefferson Randolph pretty much like his mother. Old Master wore Vaginny cloth and a red waistcoat (all the gentlemen wore red waistcoats in dem days) and small clothes; arter dat he used to wear red breeches too.[34] Governor Page used to come up there to Monticello, wife and daughter wid him. Drove four-in-hand, servants John, Molly, and a postilion. Patrick Henry visited Old Master – coach and two, his face for all the world like the images of Bonaparte. Would stay a week or more.[35] Mann Page used to be at Monticello – a plain mild-looking man – his wife and daughter along with him. Dr. Thomas Walker lived about ten miles from Monticello—a thin-faced man. John Walker (of Belvoir), his brother, owned a great many black people.[36]

Old Master was never seen to come out before breakfast—about 8 o'clock. If it was warm weather he wouldn't ride out till evening:[37] studied upstairs till bell ring for dinner.[38] When writing he had a copyin' machine.[39] While he was a-writin' he wouldn't suffer nobody to come in his room. Had a dumb-waiter; when he wanted anything he had nothin' to do but turn a crank and the dumb-waiter would bring him water or fruit on a plate or anything he wanted.[40] Old Master had abundance of books; sometimes would have twenty of 'em down on the floor at once—read fust one, then tother. Isaac has often wondered how Old Master came to have such a mighty head; read so many of them books; and when they go to him to ax him anything, he go right straight to the book and tell you all about it.[41] He talked French and Italian. Madzay talked with him; his place was called Colle.[42] General Redhazel (Riedesel) stayed there.[43] He (Mazzei) lived at Monticello with Old Master some time. Didiot, a Frenchman, married his daughter Peggy, a heavy chunky looking woman—mighty handsome. She had a daughter Frances and a son Francis; called the daughter Franky. Mazzei brought to Monticello Antonine, Jovanini, Francis, Modena, and Belligrini, all gardeners. My Old Master's garden was monstrous large: two rows of palings, all 'round ten feet high.[44]

Mr. Jefferson had a clock in his kitchen at Monticello; never went into the kitchen except to wind up the clock.[45] He never would have less than eight covers at dinner if nobody at table but himself.[46] Had from eight to thirty-two covers for dinner. Plenty of wine, best old Antigua rum and cider; very fond of wine and water. Isaac never heard of his being disguised in drink.[47] He kept three fiddles; played in the arternoons and sometimes arter supper.[48] This was in his early time. When he begin to git so old, he didn't play. Kept a spinnet made mostly in shape of a harpsichord; his daughter played on it.[49] Mr. Fauble, a Frenchman that lived at Mr. Walker's, a music man, used to come to Monticello and tune it.[50] There was a *fortepiano* and a guitar there. Never seed anybody play on them but the French people. Isaac never could git acquainted with them; could hardly larn their names. Mr. Jefferson always singing when ridin' or walkin'; hardly see him anywhar outdoors but what he was a-singin'. Had a fine clear voice; sung minnits (minuets) and sich; fiddled in the parlor.[51] Old Master very kind to servants.

The fust year Mr. Jefferson was elected President, he took Isaac on to Philadelphia. He was then about fifteen years old; traveled on horseback in company with a Frenchman named Joseph Rattiff and Jim Hemings, a body servant. Fust day's journey they went from Monticello to old Nat Gordon's, on the Fredericksburg road, next day to Fredericksburg, then to Georgetown, crossed the Potomac there, and so to Philadelphia—eight days a-goin'. Had two ponies and Mr. Jefferson's tother riding horse Odin. Mr. Jefferson went in the phaeton. Bob Hemings drove; changed horses on the road. When they got to Philadelphia, Isaac stayed three days at Mr. Jefferson's house. Then he was bound prentice to one Bringhouse, a tinner; he lived in the direction of the Waterworks. Isaac remembers seeing the image of a woman thar holding a goose in her hand—the water spouting out of the goose's mouth. This was at the head of Market Street. Bringhouse was a short, mighty small, neat-made man; treated Isaac very well. Went thar to larn the tinner's trade. Fust week larnt to cut out and sodder; make little pepper boxes and graters and sich, out of scraps of tin, so as not to waste any till he had larnt. Then to making cups. Every Sunday Isaac would go to the President's house—large brick house, many windows; same house Ginral Washington lived in before when he was President. Old Master used to talk to me mighty free and ax me, "How you come on Isaac, larnin de tin business?" As soon as he could make cups pretty well, he carred three or four to show him. Isaac made four dozen pint cups a day and larnt to tin copper and sheets (sheet iron) —make 'em tin. He lived four years with Old Bringhouse. One time Mr. Jefferson sent to Bringhouse to tin his copper kittles and pans for kitchen use; Bringhouse sent Isaac and another prentice thar—a white boy named Charles; can't think of his other name. Isaac was the only black boy in Bringhouse's shop. When Isaac carred the cups to his Old Master to show him, he was mightily pleased. Said, "Isaac you are larnin mighty fast; I bleeve I must send you back to Vaginny to car on the tin business. You is growin too big; no use for you to stay here no longer."[52]

Arter dat Mr. Jefferson sent Isaac back to Monticello to car on the tin business thar. Old Master bought a sight of tin for the purpose. Mr. Jefferson had none of his family with him in Philadelphia. Polly, his daughter, stayed with her Aunt Patsy Carr; she lived seven or eight miles from Old Master's great house. Sam Carr was Mr. Jefferson's sister's child. There were three brothers of the Carrs—Sam, Peter, and Dabney. Patsy Jefferson, while her father was President in Philadelphia, stayed with Mrs. Eppes at Wintopoke.[53] Mrs. Eppes was a sister of Mrs. Jefferson—mightily like her sister. Frank Eppes was a big heavy man.

Old Master's servants at Philadelphia was Bob and Jim Hemings, Joseph Rattiff, a Frenchman, the hostler. Mr. Jefferson used to ride out on horseback in Philadelphia. Isaac went back to Monticello. When the tin came they fixed up a shop. Jim Bringhouse came on to Monticello all the way with Old Master to fix up the shop and start Isaac to work. Jim Bringhouse stayed thar more than a month.[54]

Isaac knew old Colonel (Archibald) Cary mighty well—as dry a looking man as ever you see in your life. He has given Isaac more whippings than he has fingers and toes. Mr. Jefferson used to set Isaac to open gates for Colonel Cary. There was three gates to open: the furst bout a mile from the house; tother one three quarters; then the yard gate at the stable three hundred yards from the house. Isaac had to open the gates. Colonel Cary would write to Old Master what day he was coming. Whenever Isaac missed opening them gates in time, the Colonel soon as he git to the house look about for him and whip him with his horse-whip. Old Master used to keep dinner for Colonel Cary. He was a tall thin-visaged man jist like Mr. Jefferson. He drove four-in-hand. The Colonel as soon as he git out of his carriage walk right straight into the kitchen and ax de cooks what they hab for dinner. If they didn't have what he wanted, bleeged to wait dinner till it was cooked. Colonel Cary made freer at Monticello than he did at home; whip anybody. Would stay several weeks; give servants money, some-times five or six dollars among 'em.[55] Tuckahoe Tom Randolph married Colonel Cary's daughter Nancy.[56] The Colonel lived at Ampthill on the James River where Colonel Bob Temple lived arterwards. Edgehill was the seat of Tom Mann Randolph, father of Jeffer-son Randolph; it was three miles from Monticello.[57]

Isaac carred on the tin business two years. It failed. He then carred on the nail business at Monticello seven years—made money at that.[58] Mr. Jefferson had the first (nail) cutting machine 'twas said, that ever was in Vaginny—sent over from England. Made wrought nails and cut nails, to shingle and lath. Sold them out of the shop. Got iron rods from Philadelphia by water; boated them up from Richmond to Milton,[59] a small town on the Rivanna; wagoned from thar.

Thomas Mann Randolph had ten children.[60] Isaac lived with him fust and last twenty-six or seven years. Treated him mighty well—one of the finest masters in Virginia. His wife a mighty peaceable woman; never holler for servant; make no fuss nor racket; pity she ever died! Tom Mann Randolph's eldest daughter

Ann, a son named Jefferson, another James, and another Benjamin. Jefferson Randolph married Mr. Nicholas' daughter. Billy Giles courted Miss Polly, Old Master's daughter. Isaac one morning saw him talking to her in the garden, right back of the nail factory shop; she was lookin on de ground. All at once she wheeled round and come off. *That* was the time she turned him off. Isaac never so sorry for a man in all his life—sorry because everybody thought that she was going to marry him. Mr. Giles give several dollars to the servants, and when he went away dat time he never come back no more.[61] His servant Arthur was a big man. Isaac wanted Mr. Giles to marry Miss Polly. Arthur always said that he was a mighty fine man. He was very rich; used to come to Monticello in a monstrous fine gig—mighty few gigs in dem days with plated mountin's and harness.

Elk Hill: Old Master had a small brick house there where he used to stay, about a mile from Elk Island on the north side of the James River.[62] The river forks there: one half runs one side of the island, tother the other side. When Mr. Jefferson was Governor, he used to stay thar a month or sich a matter; and when he was at the mountain, he would come and stay a month or so and then go back again. Blenheim was a low, large wooden house two stories high, eight miles from Monticello. Old Colonel Carter lived thar; had a light-red head like Mr. Jefferson. Isaac know'd him and every son he had. Didn't know his daughters.

Mr. Jefferson used to hunt squirrels and partridges; kept five or six guns. Oftentimes carred Isaac wid him.

Old Master wouldn't shoot partridges settin'. Said "he wouldn't take advantage of 'em"—would give 'em a chance for thar life. Wouldn't shoot a hare settin', nuther; skeer him up fust.[63] My Old Master was neat a hand as ever you see to make keys and locks and small chains, iron and brass. He kept all kind of blacksmith and carpenter tools in a great case with shelves to it in his library, an upstairs room. Isaac went up thar constant; been up thar a thousand times; used to car coal up thar. Old Master had a couple of small bellowses up thar.[64]

The likeness of Mr. Jefferson in Linn's *Life,* according to Isaac, is not much like him. Old Master never dat handsome in dis world; dat likeness right between Old Master and Ginral Washington. Old Master was square-shouldered.[65] For amusement he would work sometimes in the garden for half an hour at a time in right good earnest in the cool of the evening. Never know'd him to go out anywhar before breakfast.

The school at Monticello was in the outchamber fifty yards off from the great house on the same level. But the scholars went into the house to Old Master to git lessons, in the south end of the house called the South Octagon.[66] Mrs. Skipper (Skipwith) had two daughters thar; Mrs. Eppes, one.[67]

Mr. Jefferson's sister Polly married old Ned Bolling of Chesterfield, about ten miles from Petersburg.[68] Isaac has been thar since his death; saw the old man's grave. Mr. John Bradley owns the place now. Isaac slept in the outchamber where the scholars was; slept on the floor in a blanket; in the winter season git up in

1. Isaac Jefferson in the 1840's. (Alderman Library, University of Virginia)

the mornin' and make fire for them. From Monticello you can see mountains all round as far as the eye can reach; sometimes see it rainin' down this course and the sun shining over the tops of the clouds. Willis' Mountain sometimes looked in the cloud like a great house with two chimneys to it—fifty miles from Monticello.[69]

Thar was a sight of pictures at Monticello, pictures of Ginral Washington and the Marcus Lafayette.[70] Isaac saw him fust in the old war in the mountain with Old Master; saw him again the last time he was in Vaginny. He gave Isaac a guinea. Isaac saw him in the Capitol at Richmond and talked with him and made him sensible when he fust saw him in the old war.[71] Thar was a large marble at Monticello with twelve angels cut on it that came from Heaven—all cut in marble.[72]

About the time when my Old Master begun to wear spectacles, he was took with a swellin' in his legs; used to bathe 'em and bandage 'em; said it was settin' too much. When he'd git up and walk it wouldn't hurt him. Isaac and John Hemings nursed him two months; had to car him about on a han'barrow.[73] John Hemings went to the carpenter's trade same year Isaac went to the blacksmith's.[74] Miss Lucy, Old Master's daughter, died quite a small child; died down the country at Mrs. Eppes's or Mrs. Bolling's, one of her young aunts.[75] Old Master was embassador to France at that time. He brought a great many clothes from France with him: a coat of blue cloth trimmed with gold lace; cloak trimmed so too. Dar say it weighed fifty pounds. Large buttons on the coat as big as half a dollar; cloth set in the button; edge shine like gold. In summer he war silk coat, pearl buttons.

Colonel Jack Harvie owned Belmont, jinin' Monticello. Four as big men as any in Petersburg could git in his waistcoat. He owned Belvidere, near Richmond; the Colonel died thar. Monstrous big man. The washerwoman once buttoned his waistcoat on Isaac and three others. Mrs. Harvie was a little woman.

Mr. Jefferson never had nothing to do with horse racing or cockfighting; bought two race horses once, but not in their racing day; bought 'em arter done runnin'.[76] One was Brimmer, a pretty horse with two white feet. When he bought him he was in Philadelphia; kept him thar. One day Joseph Rattiff the Frenchman was ridin' him in the streets of Philadelphia. Brimmer got skeered; run agin shaft of a dray and got killed.[77] Tother horse was Tarkill. In his race day they called him the Roan Colt; only race horse of a roan Isaac ever see. Old Master used him for a ridin' horse.[78] Davy Watson and Billy were German soldiers. Both workmen, both smoked pipes, and both drinkers. Drank whiskey; git drunk and sing; take a week at a time drinkin' and singin'.[79] Colonel Goode of Chesterfield was a great racer. Used to visit Mr. Jefferson. Had a trainer named Pompey.

Old Master had a great many rabbits. Made chains for the old buck rabbits to keep them from killin' the young ones. Had a rabbit house (a warren) —a long rock house. Some of 'em white, some blue; they used to burrow underground. Isaac expects thar is plenty of 'em bout dar yit; used to eat 'em at Monticello.[80] Mr. Jefferson never danced nor played cards.[81] He had dogs named Ceres, Bull, Armandy, and Claremont; most of 'em French dogs; he brought 'em over with him from France. Bull and Ceres were bulldogs. He brought over Buzzy with him too; she pupped at sea: Armandy and Claremont, stump tails, both black.[82]

John Brock, the overseer that lived next to the great house, had greyhounds to hunt deer.[83] Mr. Jefferson had a large park at Monticello—built in a sort of a flat on the side of the mountain. When the hunters run the deer down thar, they'd jump into the park and couldn't git out. When Old Master heard hunters in the park, he used to go down thar wid his gun and order 'em out. The park was two or three miles round and fenced in with a high fence, twelve rails double-staked and ridered. Kept up four or five years arter Old Master was gone. Isaac and his father (George) fed the deer at sunup and sundown; called 'em up and fed 'em wid corn. Had holes all along the fence at the feedin' place. Gave 'em salt; got right gentle; come up and eat out of your hand.[84]

No wildcats at Monticello; some lower down at Buck Island. Bears sometimes came on the plantation at Monticello. Wolves so plenty that they had to build pens round black peoples' quarters and pen sheep in 'em to keep the wolves from catching them. But they killed five or six of a night in the winter season; come and steal in the pens in the night. When the snow was on the groun', you could see the wolves in gangs runnin' and howlin', same as a drove of hogs; made the deer run up to the feedin' place many a night.[85] The feedin' place was right by the house whar Isaac stayed. They raised many sheep and goats at Monticello.

The woods and mountains was often on fire. Isaac has gone out to help to put out the fire. Everybody would turn out from Charlottesville and everywhere; git in the woods and sometimes work all night fightin' the fire.

Colonel Cary of Chesterfield schooled Old Master; he went to school to old Mr. Wayles. Old Master had six sisters: Polly married a Bolling; Patsy married old Dabney Carr in the low grounds; one married William Skipwith; Nancy married old Hastings Marks.[86] Old Master's brother, Mass Randall, was a mighty simple man: used to come out among black people, play the fiddle and dance half the night; hadn't much more sense than Isaac.[87] Jack Eppes that married Miss Polly lived at Mount Black on James River and then at Edgehill, then in Cumberland at Millbrooks.[88] Isaac left Monticello four years before Mr. Jefferson died.[89] Tom Mann Randolph, that married Mr. Jefferson's daughter, wanted Isaac to build a threshing machine at Varina. Old Henrico courthouse was thar; pulled down now. Coxendale Island (Dutch Gap) jinin' Varina was an Indian situation. When fresh come, it washed up more Indian bones than ever you see. When Isaac was a boy there want more than ten houses at Jamestown. Charlottesville then not as big as Pocahontas is now.[90] Mr. DeWitt kept tavern thar.

Isaac knowed Ginral Redhazel. He stayed at Colle,

Mr. Mazzei's place, two miles and a quarter from Monticello—a long wood house built by Mazzei's servants. The servants' house built of little saplin's of oak and hickory instead of laths; then plastered up. It seemed as if de folks in dem days hadn't sense enough to make laths. The Italian people raised plenty of vegetables; cooked the most victuals of any people Isaac ever see.

Mr. Jefferson bowed to everybody he meet; talked wid his arms folded. Gave the boys in the nail factory a pound of meat a week, a dozen herrings, a quart of molasses, and peck of meal. Give them that wukked the best a suit of red or blue; encouraged them mightily.[91] Isaac calls him a mighty good master.[92] There would be a great many carriages at Monticello at a time, in particular when people was passing to the Springs.

[Isaac is now (1847) at Petersburg, Virginia, seventy large odd years old; bears his years well; is a blacksmith by trade and has his shop not far from Pocahontas bridge. He is quite pleased at the idea of having his life written and protests that every word of it is true; that is, of course, according to the best of his knowledge and belief. Isaac is rather tall, of strong frame, stoops a little, in color ebony; sensible, intelligent, pleasant; wears large circular ironbound spectacles and a leather apron. A capital daguerreotype of him was taken by a Mr. Shew. Isaac was so much pleased with it that he had one taken of his wife, a large, fat, round-faced, good-humored-looking black woman. My attention was first drawn to Isaac by Mr.

Dandridge Spotswood, who had often heard him talk about Mr. Jefferson and Monticello.

C. C.

P.S. Isaac died a few years after these his recollections were taken down. He bore a good character.]

Genealogical Tables

A   Isaac's Immediate Family

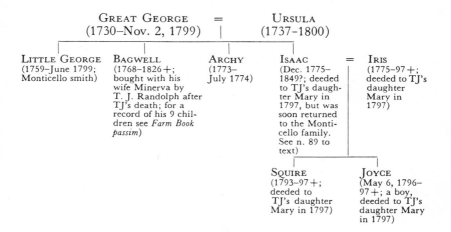

GREAT GEORGE   =   URSULA
(1730–Nov. 2, 1799) | (1737–1800)

LITTLE GEORGE
(1759–June 1799;
Monticello smith)

BAGWELL
(1768–1826 +;
bought with his
wife Minerva by
T. J. Randolph after
TJ's death; for a
record of his 9 chil-
dren see *Farm Book
passim*)

ARCHY
(1773–
July 1774)

ISAAC   =   IRIS
(Dec. 1775–   (1775–97 +;
1849?; deeded   deeded to TJ's
to TJ's daugh-   daughter
ter Mary in   Mary in
1797, but was   1797)
soon returned
to the Monti-
cello family.
See n. 89 to
text)

SQUIRE
(1793–97 +;
deeded to
TJ's daughter
Mary in 1797)

JOYCE
(May 6, 1796–
97 +; a boy,
deeded to TJ's
daughter Mary
in 1797)

A plus sign after a year indicates that the individual lived beyond that year.

B The Hemings Family

Betty Hemings[1]
(ca. 1735–1807)

MARY	MARTIN	BETT	NANCE	ROBERT[2]	JAMES[2]
(1753–92+; pastry cook, sold in 1792 to Col. Thos. Bell)	(1755/6–1807; trusted house servant)	(1759–1827+; seamstress at Monticello; called "Betty Brown")	(1761–1827+; "Old woman of no value" in 1827)	(1762–1819; in Paris with TJ; a barber; freed in 1794, called "Bob")	(1765–96; Monticello cook; freed in 1796)

BILLY
(1780–179?)

DANIEL	MOLLY	JOE	BETSY
(1772–83+)	(1777–1790+; deeded to Martha and T.M. Randolph, Jr., in 1790)	(1780–1827+; blacksmith, called "Joe Fosset"; freed under TJ's will)	(1783–Aug. 1857; given to Mary, TJ's daughter in 1797)

BILLY	WORMLEY	BURWELL[2]	BROWN	MELINDA	EDWIN	ROBERT	MARY
(1777–78; died in infancy)	(1781–1851+ gardener; dug TJ's grave)	(1783–1827+; TJ's faithful servant; freed under TJ's will)[2]	(1785–1806; nailmaker)	(1787–97+; deeded to TJ's daughter Mary in 1797)	(1793–1816+; given to T.J. Randolph)	(1799–1817?)	(1801–1827+)

[1] Betty Hemings' twelve children presumably had four fathers. Her name, Hemings, came to her from her father, an English sea captain; her mother was a full-blooded African slave of John Wayles, TJ's father-in-law.

[2] For details concerning the manumission of Robert and James Hemings, consult the *Farm Book*, 15–16, and for John, Burwell, Madison, and Eston the Appendix of the present work.

THENIA	CRITTA	PETER	SALLY	JOHN[2]	LUCY
(1767–95+; sold to Jas. Monroe in 1794)	(1769–1827+)	(1770–1827+; living with wife and 5 children in 1810; these unidentified)	(1773–1835; to Paris with Mary Jefferson; freed after 1827)	(1775–1830+ Monticello carpenter; freed under TJ's will; married but family un-identified)	(1777–86; death reported to TJ in Paris)
	JAMEY (Apr. 3, 1787–1812+. Called Jamey Hubbard; ran away in 1804 and 1812; sold to Reuben Perry in 1812)				
	HARRIET (1795–97)	BEVERLEY (1798–1822+; ran away in 1822)	HARRIET (1802–22+; spinner and weaver; ran away in 1822 and then freed by TJ)	MADISON[2] (1805–73+; carpenter; trained by his uncle, John; freed under TJ's will; married in 1830; moved to Ohio in 1836; left his recollections)	ESTON[2] (1808–54?; freed under TJ's will; moved to Ohio in 1830 with brother, Madison; later to Wisconsin in 1852)

JEFFERSON AT MONTICELLO
The Private Life of Thomas Jefferson

I

Introduction to Captain Bacon

"THOMAS JEFFERSON still survives!" were the dying
words of the elder Adams. At that moment the devoted
family and friends, at Monticello and at Quincy, were
moving with the same noiseless tread, and watching
with the same breathless interest, the closing scenes in
the lives of those illustrious men. Adams and Jefferson
breathed their last, July 4, 1826; and the waves of grief
from Quincy and Monticello soon intermingled and
overspread the land. The nation was in tears. Adams
and Jefferson were no more. The one by his tongue,
the other by his pen, had done more than any others,
by these means, to secure the liberty and independence
of their country. That country had lavished upon each
her highest honors; and, as if in approval of their life-
work, Heaven had kindly ordained that both should
die upon the anniversary of that day that they had done
so much to make immortal.

These pages are devoted especially to the memory of
Jefferson. The dying utterance of the sage of Quincy
was not less the statement of a fact, than a prophecy.
Thomas Jefferson still survives. Thomas Jefferson will
survive so long as our country or its history endures.
That he was the author of the Declaration of Independence; that he filled the highest posts of public
trust at home and abroad; that his name and influence
are interwoven with the early history of his state and

country; that he was the founder of the University of Virginia; these facts, and such as these, are well known to all. In all these relations, Thomas Jefferson still survives in history and in the universal knowledge of his countrymen.

But it will doubtless be new to most of my readers that Thomas Jefferson still survives in all the minutest details of his every-day home life at Monticello; as a farmer, manufacturer, and master; as a lover of fine horses, hogs, and sheep; as the enthusiastic cultivator of fruits and flowers; as the kind neighbor, the liberal benefactor of the poor, the participator in the childish sports of his grandchildren, the hospitable entertainer of swarms of visitors that well-nigh ate up all his substance and consumed his life—in all these, and numerous other relations, Thomas Jefferson still survives in the iron memory and in the most devoted and tender affection and veneration of a now-aged man, who was for twenty years the chief overseer and business manager of his estate at Monticello. Such is the fact.

On a visit, some months since with one of my associates, to a neighborhood in Trigg County, Kentucky, about twenty miles from my own home, our host, Captain C. W. Roach, remarked: "I have a near neighbor, Captain Edmund Bacon, who lived with Thomas Jefferson at Monticello, as overseer, for twenty years."

"We should be most happy to go and see him," was our response, and very soon we were on our way. Most naturally, as we rode on, our conversation turned on the distinguished men that Virginia had given to the country and the world. Though I doubt not my readers are as impatient for the introduction that was before us as we were, I am sure they will pardon me for detaining them with some of the details of that conversation.

Captain Roach was a native of Charlotte County, Virginia, the home of John Randolph. He had been familiar with his appearance from childhood, had frequently heard him speak, had often seen him driving about the country with four magnificent blooded horses to his carriage, and his servants following him with perhaps a dozen more equally "high-bred" and fiery. He gave us a number of anecdotes illustrating his eccentricities. One of these was so very characteristic of the man, that I must repeat it.

A Baptist clergyman, the Rev. Abner W. Clopton, took charge of some Baptist churches in Charlotte County and attracted unusual attention as a preacher. He had been a professor in the University of North Carolina, at Chapel Hill, and the fame of his learning and eloquence drew large crowds to hear him.[1] Mr. Randolph, whose solicitude for his servants is well known, employed Mr. Clopton to preach to them and generally attended these services. On one occasion, having been particularly moved by the sermon, he arose at its close and commenced an address to his sable audience. As he proceeded, his feelings became deeply enlisted, and in the most appropriate, beautiful, and eloquent manner, he urged upon them the importance of the great moral truths that the preacher had presented to them. Mr. Clopton told Captain Roach, a few days after, that no clergyman could have spoken more appropriately or beautifully. In conclusion, he expressed his great gratification at seeing them there, said he was very glad to provide preaching for them, was willing and anxious to afford them all the religious privileges they could desire, *except night meetings*. He could not and would not tolerate them. He grew indignant and bitter as he went on to speak of their evil effects and said there was nothing that he hated worse, unless it was a mean, thieving overseer, to whom, in his indignation, he applied another and much stronger epithet, not at all in keeping with the moral lecture he had just given. As quick as thought he set about extricating himself from the awkward condition into which he had been led by his passions, and very deliberately went on to say, "Now if there were any common, vulgar people here, they would perhaps go away and say that I had used profane language; but my clerical friend here, who is a fine classical scholar, knows that 'damned' means condemned; and therefore I simply mean to say an overseer that everybody condemns."

As we approached our destination, I remarked to Captain Roach that as it was so late in the afternoon we should have but a short time to stay, and I was anxious to spend as little time as possible in general conversation, so that we might hear as much as possible of Mr. Jefferson from one who had been with him so many years and must have known him so well.

"Give yourself no uneasiness about that," said he. "Captain Bacon is enthusiastic and entirely at home on two subjects, and he never tires of talking about either.

One is Thomas Jefferson, and the other is fine horses; and he easily passes from one to the other. We shall not be in the house many minutes before you will be certain to hear something of Mr. Jefferson."

We entered the house and were introduced to Captain Bacon as connected with the college at Princeton.[2] The form of our introduction was most fortunate. It was pivotal. To Captain Bacon's mind the mention of a college most naturally suggested the University of Virginia, and Mr. Jefferson's labors and solicitude in its behalf. He began at once to give the early history of the institution, and we soon found not only that he could talk about Mr. Jefferson, but that he was an uncommonly interesting talker, as the reader shall have occasion to see, for my pencil was soon in requisition.

"You know," said he, "that Mr. Jefferson was the founder of the University of Virginia. Let me see if I can remember all the Commissioners. There were Mr. Jefferson, Mr. Madison, Mr. Monroe, Chapman Johnson, John H. Cocke, and some others. They are all that I now remember. The act of the Legislature, if I mistake not, made it their duty to establish the University within a mile of the courthouse at Charlottesville. They advertised for proposals for a site.[3] Three men offered sites, Nicholas Lewis, John H. Craven, and John M. Perry. The Commissioners had a meeting at Monticello and then went and looked at all these sites. After they had made this examination, Mr. Jefferson sent me to each of them, to request them to send by me their price, which was to be sealed up."

"Do you remember the different prices?" said I.

"I think I do. Lewis and Craven each asked $17 per acre, and Perry $12. That was a mighty big price in those days. I went to Craven and Lewis first. When I went to Perry, he inquired of me if I knew what price the others had asked. I told him I did, but I did not think it would be right for me to tell him. They had both talked the matter over with me, and told me what they were a-going to ask. But I told Perry that if he asked about $10 or $12 per acre, I thought he would be mighty apt to succeed. They took Perry's forty acres, at $12 per acre. It was a poor old turned-out field, though it was finely situated.[4] Mr. Jefferson wrote the deed himself, and I carried it to Mr. Perry, and he signed it. Afterwards Mr. Jefferson bought a large tract near it from a man named Avery. It had a great deal of fine timber and rock on it, which was used in building the University.[5]

"My next instruction was to get ten able-bodied hands to commence the work. I soon got them, and Mr. Jefferson started from Monticello to lay off the foundation and see the work commenced. An Irishman named Dinsmore and I went along with him. As we passed through Charlottesville, I went to old Davy Isaacs' store and got a ball of twine, and Dinsmore found some shingles and made some pegs, and we all went on to the old field together. Mr. Jefferson looked over the ground some time and then stuck down a peg. He stuck the very first peg in that building, and then directed me where to carry the line, and I stuck the second. He carried one end of the line, and I the other, in laying off the foundation of the University. He had a little rule in his pocket that he always carried with him, and with this he measured off the ground and laid off the entire foundation, and then set the men at work.[6] I have that rule now, and here it is," said Captain Bacon, taking it from a drawer in his secretary that he unlocked, to show it to us. It was a small twelve-inch rule, so made as to be but three inches long when folded up. "Mr. Jefferson and I were once going along the bank of the canal," said he, "and in crawling through some bushes and vines, it fell out of his pocket and slid down the bank into the river. Some time after that, when the water had fallen, I went and found it and carried it to Mr. Jefferson. He told me I had had a great deal of trouble to get it, and as he had provided himself with another, I could keep it. I intend to keep it as long as I live; and when I die, that rule can be found locked up in that drawer.

"After the foundation was nearly completed, they had a great time laying the cornerstone. The old field was covered with carriages and people. There was an immense crowd there. Mr. Monroe laid the cornerstone. He was President at that time. He held the instruments and pronounced it square. He only made a few remarks, and Chapman Johnson and several others made speeches. Mr. Jefferson—poor old man!—I can see his white head just as he stood there and looked on.[7]

"After this he rode there from Monticello every day while the University was building, unless the weather was very stormy. I don't think he ever missed a day unless the weather was *very* bad.[8] Company never made any difference. When he could not go on account of the weather, he would send me, if there was anything he wanted to know. He looked after all the materials and would not allow any poor materials to go into the building if he could help it. He took as much pains in seeing that everything was done right as if it had been his own house."

After answering a great many questions in regard to Mr. Jefferson, Captain Bacon said he had a great many of his letters and proposed to show us a specimen of his handwriting. He unlocked a drawer and brought us a paper, which most naturally he prizes very highly, of which the following is a copy:

> Warm Springs, Aug. 18, 1818
> The bearer, Mr. Edmund Bacon, has lived with me twelve years as manager of my farm at Monticello. He goes to the Missouri to look out for lands to which he means to remove. He is an honest, correct man in his conduct, and worthy of confidence in his engagements. Any information or instruction which any person may give him, will be worthily bestowed; and if he should apply particularly to Gov. Clark on his way, the Governor will especially oblige me by imparting to him his information and advice.
>
> THOMAS JEFFERSON

Mr. Bacon has continued to possess the esteem, confidence and good-will of his neighbors, and of the family in which he has lived, without any interruption to this day.

> TH. M. RANDOLPH

September 14, 1820

I will here add that Captain Bacon has now resided in Kentucky about forty years, and his neighbors, who have known him during all that time, would vouch as strongly for his character as Mr. Jefferson and his son-in-law, Governor Randolph, have done. He is a man of wealth and character.

Our time was exhausted, and expressing our great gratification at our visit, we arose to leave; but Captain Bacon insisted that we should go to his stable and see his horses. He had two of them brought out and exhibited for our gratification. They were magnificent specimens of that noble animal. Their pedigrees for an indefinite period backward were at his tongue's end, and he showed a knowledge of blooded horses that I think would have astonished any old Virginia connoisseur in that line. He was certainly thoroughly Jeffersonian in his love for fine horses. He had taken the leading stock journals of the country for more than fifty years and seemed to know all about all the most noted horses there had been in the country in all that time. Like Mr. Jefferson, he has never patronized nor in any way encouraged horse racing. He says that though John Randolph had sometimes a hundred* blooded

---

* Charlotte County, Va., May 19, 1826

. . . Mr. Randolph is the Magnus Apollo of this county. Every one knows and fears him. His power of sarcasm and invective is such, that no one pretends to contradict him. He has three several plantations in this county, all of them extensive. His horses (I mean those which are never used) are worth, I suppose, about $8,000.

Charlotte, April 10, 1827

. . . This part of Virginia has long been celebrated for its breed of horses. There is a scrupulous attention paid to the preservation of the immaculate English blood. Among the crowd on this day were snorting and rearing fourteen or fifteen stallions, some of which were indeed fine specimens of that noble creature. Among the rest, Mr. Randolph's celebrated English horse Roanoke, who is nine years

horses, the finest stable of horses in Virginia, he never trained them for the turf—never allowed them to race.

On leaving, I told Captain Bacon that if my life was spared that would not be my last visit to him. I felt that I had found a rich historical *placer* that I was determined to thoroughly work as soon as I could find time to do so.

I have recently been able to accomplish that determination. I have spent several weeks with my host, to whom I was indebted for this introduction, and day after day I have gone to Captain Bacon's and listened to his reminiscences of his venerated employer. He was never weary of talking on this theme, nor I of listening. At his fireside, around his hospitable table, strolling among his blooded stock, and riding over his immense plantation, he poured forth from the inexhaustible storehouse of his wonderful memory the accumulations of a score of the best years of his life, that were spent at Monticello. It will be my object in the pages that follow, to give the results of these conversations. I shall not trouble the reader with the thousand questions I have asked but will give the answers in narrative form, as nearly as possible in Captain Bacon's own language. He has frequently remarked to me, that when he was a boy, there were no such opportunities for education as now; that he had only an "old-field-school, picked-up education"; but the reader will see that he has "picked up" a very terse, vigorous

---

old, and has never been "backed" (*Forty Years' Familiar Letters of James W. Alexander, D.D.* [New York: Scribner, 1860], 95, 101). [Pierson's note.]

use of language. This is no doubt largely due to the unconscious influence of Mr. Jefferson, for whom his admiration is most profound, and was acquired in his twenty years' correspondence and conversations with him in regard to his business affairs.

In my visits to Captain Bacon, I took notes of all that he said of Mr. Jefferson. Sometimes he would talk at length upon one subject, and at others his conversation was perfectly discursive. But wherever he went I followed him with my "notes," asking him questions and drawing him out whenever his mind seemed most excited by his own reminiscences upon particular themes. In this manner we talked and I wrote, day after day, until I had gained from him all the information I could possibly acquire in regard to Mr. Jefferson. Having in this manner filled a blank book with "notes" and having carefully looked over Captain Bacon's papers and selected, by his permission, all those in the handwriting of Mr. Jefferson, Mr. Monroe, Mr. Randolph, and some others, I returned home with my historical treasures.

In writing this volume, I have done very little "editing," except that the results of these conversations are arranged, as far as possible, under the subjects to which they appropriately belong. The reader will bear in mind that these reminiscences go back over a period of from forty to sixty years; yet in no instance has Captain Bacon referred to a manuscript or written memorandum in regard to any of the facts communicated. They are literally "reminiscences." It is therefore well-nigh impossible that there should be no inaccuracies in any of the statements. Should any reader make such a discovery, I am sure that in the circumstances he will need no exhortation from me, in behalf of my aged friend, to

> Be to his faults a little blind;
> Be to his virtues very kind.

Before proceeding with these reminiscences of Mr. Jefferson, it will be proper for me *more fully* to introduce Captain Bacon to my readers. This I shall do in the next chapter.

II

Bacon's Autobiography

I AM now seventy-six years old. I was born March 28, 1785, within two or three miles of Monticello, so that I recollect Mr. Jefferson as far back as I can remember anybody. My father and he were raised together and went to school together. My oldest brother, William Bacon, had charge of his estate during the four years he was Minister to France.[1] After he was elected President, he told my father he wanted an overseer, and he wished to employ my brother William again. But he was then quite an old man, and very well off, and did not wish to go. He then inquired of my father if he could not spare me. He replied that he thought I was too young. I was his youngest son and not of age yet. Mr. Jefferson requested him to send me to see him about it. My father was a comfortable farmer; had ten or twelve hands. He was very industrious and taught all his children to work. Mr. Jefferson knew this. That was why he wanted one of my father's sons. He was the most industrious man I ever knew. When my father told me Mr. Jefferson wanted to employ me, I was keen to go; and I determined that if he employed me, I would please him, if there was any such thing. When I went to see him, he told me what he wanted me to do, gave me good advice, and said he would try me and see how I would get along. I went to live with him the 27th of the December before he was inaugurated as

President; and if I had remained with him from the 8th of October to the 27th of December, the year that I left him, I should have been with him precisely twenty years.[2]

"Some time before I left him, I determined to go West and buy land upon which to settle, and Mr. Jefferson recommended me to go to the Missouri. It was a territory then, and there was a great deal of talk about it. At the time that we had arranged that I should go and look at the country, Mr. Jefferson was at the Warm Springs. In going to his Bedford farm, he had somehow caught the itch, and it troubled him a great deal, and he went to the Springs to see if he could not get rid of it. But he wrote me not to let his absence interrupt my plans and said that in going I would pass directly through the yard where he was staying, and he would see me there. That is why that letter of his, that I showed you, is dated at the Warm Springs.[3]

"There were six of us started together on horseback from Charlottesville for the Missouri, John D. Coles, Absalom Johnson, James Garnett, William Bacon, and — — Jones, I forget his given name; he was as good company as ever lived. We went by the Warm Springs, Hot Springs, Guyandotte, and crossed the Big Sandy at its mouth; and then went on by Flemingsburg, Mt. Sterling, Lexington, and Shelbyville, to Louisville. It was a little settlement then, and the people were very anxious we should settle there. When we crossed the Ohio into Indiana, there was no road at all. We took a pilot and went to Vincennes. We had no road, only a bridle path. From there we went to Edwardsville, Illinois, where Edward Coles, afterwards governor of the state, then lived.[4] I had known him well in Albemarle County; we were raised together. He was very anxious for us to buy land there. He had bought a great deal. He had taken about twenty Negroes with him from Virginia, who worked for him for a time and made improvements on his land. He finally sold his land for a great profit, freed his Negroes, and went back to Virginia. From here we went on to St. Louis.

"There were no bridges on our route, and only the large rivers, like the Ohio and Mississippi, had ferry-boats. We had to swim all the smaller streams. Some of the more difficult streams had dugout canoes, in which we rowed over and swam our horses behind and beside us. My mare was one of the best animals ever backed. She was a granddaughter of imported Diomede.[5] She would swim almost like a fish. She would seldom wet me above the knees. Garnett's horse was a poor swimmer, swam very deep. He called him Henry. When we crossed a river, you could only see his head out of the water, and Garnett would be wet almost to the armpits. On our way we saw a great deal of game–gangs of deer, fowls, and wolves. At one house where we stayed all night, the wolves came about the house and howled so terribly that the dogs were afraid of them–would not go out and attack them. They took several pigs out of the pen, and we had to go out and throw brands of fire at them to drive them away. We saw no bears except some tame ones that had been caught by the people when they were young.

"When we got to St. Louis, I called on Governor

Clark and showed him the letter from Mr. Jefferson, and I never was more kindly treated.[6] There was a small tavern near the ferry, but he insisted that I should stay with him. He knew a great deal about the Western country. He and Meriwether Lewis had explored the Missouri River. St. Louis was a dingy little settlement, not much larger than a good Negro quarter. There was only one narrow street three or four hundred yards long. The houses were mostly old-looking, built of rock in the roughest manner possible. A few of them were plastered houses. They were all one story. Governor Clark lived in a one-story plastered house with two rooms. The fences around their truck patches (gardens) were a kind of wicker-work made of posts stuck into the ground, and brush wattled into them. For miles around it was a prairie country. Back from the river some two or three miles, there was a large spring, and near it a windmill that did most of the grinding for the settlement. I went out there several times. When the wind blew hard, it ground very fast. Most of the people were French. Even the Negroes spoke French. Governor Clark was very anxious that I should buy there. He advised me to look no further. He said that with so many large rivers coming in near there and such a rich, fertile country, it must some day be a large place. He told me there was a Frenchman named Chouteau who had a great deal of land there and was very anxious to sell a thousand acres. He said the Frenchman needed everything but land. I went to see him, and Clark sent his clerk along with me to interpret. He was almost as black as a

Negro, lived in a low, squatty brick house, almost without furniture. It had benches in place of chairs. He was very anxious to sell and only asked me three dollars an acre for a thousand acres. I concluded to look further over the Territory. We got a pilot and traveled several hundred miles over the country north and south of the Missouri River and returned to St. Louis. Chouteau sent to me several times to urge me to buy of him, and Clark persuaded me to it very strongly. If I had only taken his advice! I had $3,000 in a belt around me; but by this time I had concluded I would not take off my belt and pay out my money for all the land in the Territory. You could raise abundance of everything, but could get nothing for it. There was no such thing as a steamboat on any Western river. Such a thing wasn't thought of then. Keel and flatboats were the only kind of navigation. The people told me how they did. When they had a surplus of bacon, flour, and venison, they would load up a flatboat and take it to New Orleans. It took four or five months to make the trip, and they got very little for their load. It was a solemn sight to see a boat start off. The people would assemble on the bank of the river and bid their friends farewell. It was very uncertain whether they would ever see them again, for they were going into a dead, sickly place, and they had to walk all the way back through an Indian country.

"I returned to Virginia without making any purchase, remained a few years longer with Mr. Jefferson, and then removed my family to Kentucky and rented a farm until I could look over the country and satisfy myself. I went to St. Louis and looked over the state again but could not make up my mind to settle there. Chouteau was still anxious to sell, and Clark anxious that I should buy; but I concluded that Kentucky was far enough West and that I would go back and buy there."

Could Captain Bacon have looked into the future, he would have purchased the thousand acres which are now covered by the city of St. Louis. It is now very easy to see how he missed an immense fortune. "If our foresight was as good as our hindsight, it would be an easy matter to get rich." But Captain Bacon is not particularly to be pitied in this regard. He purchased, at two dollars per acre, a thousand acres of much better farming land, where he now resides, to which he has since made additions, until he now has about four thousand acres. This, with a large amount of most valuable stock, and (as his neighbors tell me) a good many thousand dollars at interest, make a fortune so ample as to leave very little room for reasonable regret in regard to his decision at St. Louis.

Moreover, there were potent reasons for that decision. Governor Clark, in his prophetic portraiture of the brilliant future that was before St. Louis and in all his other earnest and eloquent persuasives, was opposed by pleadings that he wot not of. He was engaged in an unequal contest.

Captain Bacon was a widower. His wife had died in Kentucky. Kentucky, so famed as "the dark and bloody ground," is not less famed for the unerring execution of other than Indian archers. Many a passing traveler has received their darts—has been taken captive. Captain Bacon had seen a Kentucky widow. He shall tell the rest.

We were sitting around his large old-fashioned fireplace, as was our wont. Mrs. Bacon, who at seventy-six is hale and hearty and as active as most ladies at thirty or forty, was sitting in one "corner" by her window, busy with her knitting and absorbed with the conversation. Captain Bacon was near her, his face all aglow with his own reminiscences of long-gone years, and the writer was in the other corner, with pencil and notebook in hand. With a smile that indicated the most perfect satisfaction with the whole result, Captain Bacon gave the following "explanation" of his failure to make the St. Louis purchase:

"The fact is, sir," said he, "I believe I should have bought in St. Louis, if it had not been for the old lady here. I had seen her. The last night I was in St. Louis, I determined I would go back and marry her, if possible, and settle here. We have now lived together nearly forty years, and I believe neither of us is tired of the union or anxious to secede."

III

Monticello

CAPTAIN BACON SAYS: Monticello is quite a high mountain, in the shape of a sugar loaf.[1] A winding road led up to the mansion. On the very top of the mountain the forest trees were cut down, and ten acres were cleared and leveled off. This was done before I went to live with Mr. Jefferson. The house in the picture that you showed me is upon the highest point.[2] That picture is perfectly natural. I knew every room in that house. Under the house and the terraces that surrounded it, were his cisterns, icehouse, cellar, kitchen, and rooms for all sorts of purposes. His servants' rooms were on one side. They were very comfortable, warm in the winter and cool in the summer. Then there were rooms for vegetables, fruit, cider, wood, and every other purpose. There were no Negro and other outhouses around the mansion, as you generally see on plantations. The grounds around the house were most beautifully ornamented with flowers and shrubbery. There were walks, and borders, and flowers, that I have never seen or heard of anywhere else. Some of them were in bloom from early in the spring until late in the winter. A good many of them were foreign. Back of the house was a beautiful lawn of two or three acres, where his grandchildren used to play a great deal. His garden was on the side of the mountain.[3] I had it built mostly while he was President. It took a great deal of labor. We had to blow out the rock for the walls for the different terraces and then make the soil. I have some of the instructions that Mr. Jefferson sent me from Washington now. It was a fine garden. There were vegetables of all kinds, grapes, figs, and the greatest variety of fruit. I have never seen such a place for fruit. It was so high that it never failed. Mr. Jefferson sent home many kinds of trees and shrubbery from Washington. I used to send a servant there with a great many fine things from Monticello for his table, and he would send back the cart loaded with shrubbery from a nursery near Georgetown that belonged to a man named Maine, and he would always send me directions what to do with it.[4] He always knew all about everything in every part of his grounds and garden. He knew the name of every tree, and just where one was dead or missing. Here is a letter that he sent me from Washington:

Washington, Nov. 24, 1807

Sir,–Davy has been detained till now, the earth having been so frozen that the plants could not be dug up. On the next leaf are instructions what to do with them, in addition to which I inclose Mr. Maine's instructions as to the thorns. He brings a couple of Guinea pigs, which I wish you to take great care of, as I propose to get this kind into the place of those we have now, as I greatly prefer their size and form. I think you had better keep them in some inclosure near your house till spring. I hope my sheep are driven up every night, and carefully attended to. The finishing every thing about the mill, is what I wish always to have a preference to every kind of work. Next to that, my heart is most set on finishing the garden. I have promised Mr. Craven that nothing shall run next year in the meadow inclosure, where his clearing will be. This is necessary for ourselves, that we may mow the clover and feed it green. I have hired the same negroes for another year, and am promised them as long as I want them. Stewart must be immediately dismissed.[5] If he will do those jobs I mentioned before he goes, he may stay to do them, and have provisions while about them. Joe may work in the way you proposed, so that the whole concern may be together.[6] I place here the statement of debts and remittances:

DEBTS.

Jacob Cooper,........................	£8	1s.	6d. =	$*26 92
John Peyton,.........................	21	12	3 =	72 04
Dr. Jamieson,........................	7	10	0 =	35 00
Thomas Carr, corn,....................				35 00
Thomas Burras, 18 hogs,...............				20 75
Richard Anderson, flour,..............				13 00
John Rogers, beef and corn,...........				117 00
James Butler, flour,..................				10 00
Do. beeves,.......................				85 00
Robt. Burras, 20 barrels corn,........				35 00
Robt. Terril, 100 do.................				175 00
Do. 10,000 lbs. fodder,...........				50 00
Your own balance,....................				133 33
				$808 04

REMITTANCES.

Oct. 12.	Remitted.............................	$101	00
Nov. 9.	Do..................................	110	00
Dec. 6.	By Mr. Craven,.......................	200	00
	To the order of Kelly,...............	33	33
Jan.	I shall remit........................	260	00
Feb.	Do..................................	103	71
		$808	04

[* TJ used a *D* rather than a $ mark.]

By these remittances and payments made and to be made, you will perceive that the whole will be paid off by the first week in February. Mr. Craven called on me the 17th, with your order to pay him $100 the first week in December; but he said you would receive $200 of his money, and that he should be extremely distressed if he could not get the whole sum here.[7] On that I gave him my note to pay $200 to his order the first week of next month, and you are to use his $200 instead of what I intended to remit you at that time. Last night I received from Mr. Kelly your order to pay him $133⅓.[8] To reconcile these two transactions, you can use $100 of Craven's money towards paying the debts. Pay Mr. Kelly $100 of it, in part of your order on me, and I will remit $33⅓, according to his order, by which means every thing will be brought to rights. I shall write to him on this subject, and shall be glad to learn that this arrangement is made, and is satisfactory.

I tender you my best wishes.

TH. JEFFERSON

DIRECTIONS FOR MR. BACON[9]

If the weather is not open and soft when Davy[10] arrives, put the box of thorns into the cellar, where they may be entirely free from the influence of cold, until the weather becomes soft, when they must be planted in the places of those dead through the whole of the hedges which inclose the two orchards, so that the old and the new shall be complete, at 6 inches' distance from every plant. If any remain, plant them in the nursery of thorns. There are 2,000. I send Mr. Maine's written instructions about them, which must be followed most minutely. The other trees he brings are to be planted as follows:

4 Purple beaches. In the clumps which are in the southwest and northwest angles of the house, (which Wormley knows.) There were 4 of these trees planted

last spring, 2 in each clump. They all died, but the places will be known by the remains of the trees, or by sticks marked No. IV. in the places. I wish these now sent to be planted in the same places.

4 Robinias, or red locusts. In the clumps in the N. E. and S. E. angles of the house. There were 2 of these planted last spring, to wit, 1 in each. They are dead, and two of them are to be planted in the same places, which may be found by the remains of the trees, or by sticks marked V. The other 2 may be planted in any vacant places in the S. W. and N. W. angles.

4 Prickly ash. In the S. W. angle of the house there was planted one of these trees last spring, and in the N. W. angle 2 others. They are dead. 3 of those now sent are to be planted in their places, which may be found by the remains of the trees, or by sticks marked VII. The fourth may be planted in some vacant space of the S. W. angle.

6 Spitzenberg apple trees. Plant them in the S. E. orchard, in any place where apples have been planted and are dead.

5 Peach trees. Plant in the S. E. orchard, wherever peach trees have died.

500 October peach stones; a box of Peccan nuts. The nursery must be enlarged, and these planted in the new parts, and Mr. Perry must immediately extend the paling so as to include these, and make the whole secure against hares.

Some turfs of a particular grass. Wormley must plant them in some safe place of the orchard, where he will know them, and keep other grass from the place.

I think, *said Captain Bacon,* there were three hundred acres inclosed in the tract about the house. Mr. Jefferson would never allow a tree to be cut off from this. There were roads and paths winding all

2. Jefferson's freehand sketch of the west front of Monticello, circa 1770. (Thomas Jefferson Memorial Foundation)

3. The west front of Monticello, after a painting by George Cooke of Richmond in the 1830's. The original has been lost; the earliest copy is in the *Family Magazine*, Vol. IV (1837).

around and over it, where the family could ride and walk for pleasure.[11] How often I have seen him walking over these grounds and his grandchildren following after him as happy as they could be.

The estate was very large. I did know the exact number of acres, for I have paid the taxes a great many times. There was about ten thousand acres. It extended from the town lots of Charlottesville to beyond Milton, which was five or six miles. It was not a profitable estate; it was too uneven and hard to work. Mr. Madison's plantation was much the most profitable. It was divided into four plantations—Tuffton, Lego, Shadwell, and Pantops.[12] There was a Negro quarter and a white overseer at each of these places. A Negro named Jim was overseer of the hands at Monticello.

We used to get up a strife between the different overseers, to see which would make the largest crops, by giving premiums. The one that delivered the best crop of wheat to the hand had an extra barrel of flour; the best crop of tobacco, a fine Sunday suit; the best lot of pork, an extra hundred and fifty pounds of bacon. Negro Jim always had the best pork, so that the other overseers said it was no use for them to try any more, as he would get it anyway. An overseer's allowance of provisions for a year was pork, six hundred pounds; wheat flour, two barrels; corn meal, all they wanted. They had gardens and raised their own vegetables. The servants also had rewards for good conduct.

I had written instructions about everything, so that I always knew exactly what to do. Here are the instructions he gave me when he went to Washington:

MEMORANDUMS

The first work to be done, is to finish every thing at the mill; to wit, the dam, the stone still wanting in the south abutment, the digging for the addition to the toll mill, the waste, the dressing off the banks and hollows about the mill-houses, making the banks of the canal secure everywhere. In all these things Mr. Walker will direct what is to be done, and how.

The second job is the fence from near Nance's house to the river, the course of which will be shown. Previous to this a change in the road is to be made, which will be shown also.

As this fence will completely separate the river field from the other grounds, that field is to be cleaned up; the spots in it still in wood are to be cut down where they are not too steep for culture; a part of the field is to be planted in Quarantine corn, which will be found in a tin canister in my closet. This corn is to be in drills 5 feet apart, and the stalks 18 inches asunder in the drills. The rest of the ground is to be sown in oats, and red clover sowed on the oats. All ploughing is to be done horizontally, in the manner Mr. Randolph does his.

180 Cords of coal wood are next to be cut. The wood cut in the river field will make a part, and let the rest be cut in the flat lands on the meadow branch south of the overseer's house, which I intend for a Timothy meadow. Let the wood be all corded, that there may be no deception as to the quantity. A kiln will be wanting to be burnt before Christmas; but the rest of the wood had better lie seasoning till spring, when it will be better to burn it.

When these things are done, the levelling of the garden is to be resumed. The hands having already worked at this, they understand the work. John best knows how to finish off the levelling.

I have hired all the hands belonging to Mrs. and Miss Dangerfield, for the next year. They are nine in number. Moses the miller is to be sent home when his year is up. With these will work in common, Isaac, Charles, Ben, Shepherd, Abram, Davy, John, and Shoemaker Phill; making a gang of 17 hands. Martin is the miller, and Jerry will drive his wagon.

Those who work in the nailery, are Moses, Wormly, Jame Hubbard, Barnaby, Isbel's Davy, Bedford John, Bedford Davy, Phill Hubbard, Bartlet, and Lewis.[13] They are sufficient for 2 fires, five at a fire. I am desirous a single man, a smith, should be hired to work with them, to see that their nails are well made, and to superintend them generally; if such an one can be found for $150 or $200 a year, though I would rather give him a share in the nails made, say one-eighth of the price of all the nails made, deducting the cost of the iron; if such a person can be got, Isbel's Davy may be withdrawn to drive the mule wagon, and Sampson join the laborers. There will then be 9 nailers, besides the manager, so that 10 may still work at 2 fires; the manager to have a log house built, and to have 500 lbs. of pork. The nails are to be sold by Mr. Bacon, and the accounts to be kept by him; and he is to direct at all times what nails are to be made.

The toll of the mill is to be put away in the two garners made, which are to have secure locks, and Mr. Bacon is to keep the keys. When they are getting too full, the wagons should carry the grain to the overseer's house, to be carefully stowed away. In general, it will be better to use all the bread corn from the mill from week to week, and only bring away the surplus. Mr. Randolph is hopper-free and toll-free at the mill. Mr. Eppes having leased his plantation and gang, they are to pay toll hereafter.

Clothes for the people are to be got from Mr.

Higginbotham, of the kind heretofore got. I allow them a best striped blanket every three years. Mr. Lilly had failed in this; but the last year Mr. Freeman gave blankets to one-third of them. This year 11 blankets must be bought, and given to those most in need, noting to whom they are given. The hirelings, if they had not blankets last year, must have them this year. Mrs. Randolph always chooses the clothing for the house servants; that is to say, for Peter Hemings, Burwell, Edwin, Critta, and Sally. Colored plains are provided for Betty Brown, Betty Hemings, Nance, Ursula, and indeed all the others. The nailers, laborers, and hirelings may have it, if they prefer it to cotton. Wool is given for stockings to those who will have it spun and knit for themselves. Fish is always to be got from Richmond, by writing to Mr. Jefferson, and to be dealt out to the hirelings, laborers, workmen, and house servants of all sorts, as has been usual.

600 Lbs. of pork is to be provided for the overseer, 500 lbs. for Mr. Stewart, and 500 lbs. for the superintendent of the nailery, if one is employed; also about 900 lbs. more for the people, so as to give them half a pound a-piece once a week. This will require, in the whole, 2,000 or 2,500 lbs. After seeing what the plantation can furnish, and the 3 hogs at the mill, the residue must be purchased. In the winter, a hogshead of molasses must be provided and brought up, which Mr. Jefferson will furnish. This will afford to give a gill a-piece to everybody once or twice a week.

Joe works with Mr. Stewart; John Hemings and Lewis with Mr. Dinsmore; Burwell paints and takes care of the house. With these the overseer has nothing to do, except find them. Stewart and Joe do all the plantation work; and when Stewart gets into his idle frolics, it may sometimes be well for Moses or Isbel's Davy to join Joe for necessary work.

The servants living on the top of the mountain must have a cart-load of wood delivered at their doors once a week through the winter. The fence inclosing the grounds on the top of the mountain must be well done up. This had better be done before they begin the fence down the mountain. No animal of any kind must ever be loose within that inclosure. Mr. Bacon should not fail to come to the top of the mountain every 2 or 3 days, to see that nothing is going wrong, and that the gates are in order. Davy and Abram may patch up the old garden pales when work is going on from which they can best be spared.

The thorn hedges are to be kept clean wed at all times. Mr. Dinsmore is to be furnished with bread grain from the mill. The proportion of corn and wheat is left to his own discretion. He provides his own provisions, and for Mr. Nelson and Barry.

There is a spout across the canal near the head, which, if left as at present, will do mischief. I will give verbal directions about it.

As soon as the Aspen trees lose their leaves, take up one or two hundred of the young trees, not more than 2 or 3 feet high; tie them in bundles, with the roots well covered with straw. Young Davy being to carry Fanny to Washington, he is to take the little cart, (which must be put into the soundest order,) to take these trees on board. 3 Boxes in my study, marked to go by him and Fanny and her things. She must take corn for their meals, and provisions for themselves to Washington. Fodder they can buy on the road. I leave $6 with you, to give them to pay unavoidable expenses. If he could have 2 mules, without stopping a wagon, it would be better. They are to go as soon as the Aspen leaves fall.

The nailers are to work on the dam till finished, and then go to their shop. The verbal directions which I gave Mr. Bacon respecting Carroll's farm, will be recollected and observed.

ADDITIONAL MEMORANDUMS FOR MR. BACON

When the work at the mill is done, and the fence mended up on the top of the mountain, take as much time with your hands as will fill all the gullies in the field north of the overseer's house, (called Belfield,) with bushes, &c., so that they may be filling up by the time we are ready to clean it up. The scalded places should also be covered with bushes.

The orchard below the garden must be entirely cultivated the next year; to wit, a part in Ravenscroft pea, which you will find in a canister in my closet; a part with Irish potatoes, and the rest with cow-pea, of which there is a patch at Mr. Freeman's, to save which, great attention must be paid, as they are the last in the neighborhood.

Whiskey is wanted for the house, some for Mr. Dinsmore, and sometimes for the people. About 30 gallons will last a year. Mr. Merriwether or Mr. Rogers may perhaps each let us have some for nails, or will distil it out of our worst toll wheat.

In building the house for the nailer, there should be a partition laying off about 8 feet at one end, to keep his nails and rod in.

Get from Mr. Perry and Mr. Dinsmore, an estimate of all the nails we shall want for the house in Bedford; and when you have no orders to execute for others, let the boys be making them, and keep them separate from all others; and when the wagon goes up at Christmas, send what shall then be ready.

Mr. Higginbotham has all my transportation to and from Richmond under his care. He settles with the watermen, and pays them. I do not wish to have any accounts with them.

These rains have possibly spoiled the fodder you had agreed for. You had better see it, and if injured, look out in time for more.

Mr. Dinsmore wants Allen's plank brought up immediately. If you choose it, you can take your half beef now, killing one for that purpose, and sending the other half to the house, or to Mr. Randolph's.

IV

Mr. Jefferson's Blooded Stock

MR. JEFFERSON was very fond of all kinds of good stock. The first full-blooded Merino sheep in all that country were imported by Mr. Jefferson for himself and Mr. Madison, while he was President. They were sent by water to Fredericksburg. Mr. Jefferson wrote me to go with Mr. Madison's overseer at Montpelier, Mr. Graves, and get the sheep. He said he knew no better way to divide them than to draw for the choice, and the one who got the first choice of the bucks take the second choice of the ewes. When we got to Fredericksburg, we were greatly disappointed. The sheep were little bits of things, and Graves said he would not give his riding whip for the whole lot. There were six of them—two bucks and four ewes. He had the same instructions in regard to dividing them that I had; so I put my hand into my pocket and drew out a dollar and said, "Head or tail?" He guessed, and I got the first choice. There was a good deal of difference in the bucks, and not much in the ewes. I got the best buck. He was a little fellow, but his wool was as fine almost as cotton. When I got home, I put a notice in the paper at Charlottesville that persons who wished to improve their stock could send us two ewes, and we would keep them until the lambs were old enough to wean, and then give the owners the choice of the lambs, and they leave the other lamb and both of the ewes. We got the greatest lot of sheep—more than we wanted; two or three hundred, I think; and in a few years we had an immense flock. People came long distances to buy our full-blooded sheep. At first we sold them for fifty dollars, but they soon fell to thirty, and twenty; and before I left Mr. Jefferson, Merino sheep were so numerous, that they sold about as cheap as common ones.

Some years after, he imported, from Barbary I think, four large broad-tailed sheep.[1] I have forgotten their names. He sent these from Washington in his own wagon, which had gone there with a load from Monticello. These sheep made very fine mutton, but they were not popular—did not disseminate and ran out in a few years. About the time the first sheep were imported, Mr. Jefferson imported six hogs—a pair for himself, Mr. Madison, and General Dearborne, one of his secretaries.[2] He often visited Mr. Jefferson. He was a large, fine-looking man.[3] I remember his coming to my house once with Mr. Jefferson, to look at my bees. I had a very large stand, more than forty hives. Those imported hogs were the finest hogs I have ever known. They were called Calcutta hogs. They were black on the heads and rumps, and white-listed round the body. They were very long-bodied, with short legs; were easily kept; would live on grazing; and would scarcely ever root. They would not root much more than an ox. With common pasturage, they would weigh two hundred at a year old; and fed with corn, and well treated, they would weigh three or four hundred.

Mr. Jefferson didn't care about making money from

his imported stock. His great object was to get it widely scattered over the country, and he left all these arrangements to me. I told the people to bring three sows, and when they came for them, they might take two and leave one. In this way he soon got a large number of hogs, and the stock was scattered over that whole country. He never imported any cattle while I was with him. We could always get remarkably fine cattle from western Virginia.[4]

But the horse was Mr. Jefferson's favorite. He was passionately fond of a good horse. We generally worked mules on the plantation, but he would not ride or drive anything but a highbred horse. Bay was his preference for color. He would not have any other. After he came from Washington he had a fine carriage built at Monticello, from a model that he planned himself.[5] The woodwork, blacksmithing, and painting were all done by his own workmen. He had the plating done in Richmond. When he traveled in this carriage, he always had five horses—four in the carriage and the fifth for Burwell, who always rode behind him. Those five horses were Diomede, Brimmer, Tecumseh, Wellington, and Eagle.

Diomede was a colt of imported Diomede. John W. Eppes, who married Mr. Jefferson's second daughter, Maria, bought Diomede for him in Chesterfield County; gave £80 for him. Eppes wrote Mr. Jefferson that he had bought him, and Mr. Jefferson wrote me to send for him. When I got him home, he was poor, but I had him in fine order when Mr. Jefferson got home. He was a fine, high-formed bay horse, not as good for riding as the others but a fine harness horse. He became blind, poor fellow.

Brimmer was a son of imported Knowlsby. He was a bay, but a shade darker than any of the others. He was a horse of fair size, full, but not quite as tall as Eagle. He was a good riding horse and excellent for the harness. Mr. Jefferson broke all his horses to both ride and work. I bought Brimmer of General John H. Cocke, of Fluvanna County; don't remember what I gave for him. General Cocke was often at Monticello. He used to ride a fine bay stallion called Roebuck that he had rode in the War of 1812. Sometimes, when he visited Monticello, he would send him to my house, because he had rather trust him with me than with the servants.

Tecumseh. I bought him of old Davy Isaacs, a Jew, who kept a store in Charlottesville. Mr. Jefferson saw him in the field several times as he was riding past, and he told me he was very much pleased with him, and he wished I would make some inquiries about him. I told him that I knew the horse and his stock well. He sent me to buy him. He was a fine horse, but tricky. He would scare at a rock, or when a bird flew up, and jump suddenly. Mr. Jefferson got a blind made that he could attach to his bridle when he rode or drove him, and in this way pretty much cured him.

Wellington. I bought him out of an Augusta County wagon, of a man named Imboden, a Dutchman. Gave £60 for him. He did not know his value. He was a large bay horse and matched Diomede. He rode better than Diomede, but not as well as the other two.

Eagle. The last thing I ever did for poor old Mr. Jefferson was to buy Eagle for him for a riding horse. The last time he ever rode on horseback, he rode Eagle; and the last letter I ever got from Mr. Jefferson, he described that ride and how Eagle fell with him in the river and lamed his wrist. I am very sorry I have lost that letter. I bought Eagle of Captain John Graves, of Louisa County. He was a bay, with white hind ankles and a white spot on his nose; full sixteen hands high and the finest sort of a riding horse.[6]

In his new carriage, with fine harness, those four horses made a splendid appearance. He never trusted a driver with lines. Two servants rode on horseback, and each guided his own pair. About once a year Mr. Jefferson used to go in his carriage to Montpelier and spend several days with Mr. Madison; and every summer he went to Poplar Forest, his farm in Bedford, and spent two or three months.[7]

Mr. Jefferson always knew all about all his stock, as well as everything else at Monticello, and gave special directions about it all. Here is one of his letters:

The sorrel riding-horse is to be kept for Mr. Bacon's riding. If Arcturus has not been exchanged for Mr. Smithson's mare, I wish him and the Chickasaw mare to be disposed of immediately. I think $150 might be expected from him, and $100 for her; but I would take a fair wagon horse or mule for either, rather than keep them. For Arcturus we ought certainly to get a first-rate wagon horse or mule. I would prefer a mule to a horse in both cases, provided they were large and docile.

Jerry and his wagon are to go to Bedford before

Christmas, and to stay there till they have done all the hauling for my house there. He is to start on the morning of Saturday, the 20th of December, and take with him a bull calf from Mr. Randolph, and the young ram which we have saved for that purpose. He is to proceed to my brother's the first day, and stay there the Sunday. He will take in there some things lodged there last year; to wit, a pair of fowls, some clover seed, and some cow-peas, and proceed with them to Poplar Forest. I promised the friends of the nailers who came from Bedford, to let the boys go and see them this winter; to wit, Jame Hubbard, Phill Hubbard, Bedford John, and Davy. They are to go with the wagon, and assist in conducting the bull and ram. They are to be at home the evening of New Year's day.

In all cases of doubt, ask the advice and direction of Mr. Randolph, who will be kind enough to give it.

If any beeves remain after I am gone, drive them to Mr. Randolph's, for his use. I should like to have 3 or 4 good milch cows bought, now giving full milk, for the use of the overseer, and people of every description. They should be such as would make good beeves next autumn.

Wormley must cover the fig bushes with straw rope.

TH. JEFFERSON

Sept. 29, '06

V

Mr. Jefferson's Manufactories

MR. JEFFERSON'S neighbors were very anxious that he should build a flouring mill. There was a small one there, but a large one was very much needed. While he was President, they thought he had a large salary and that he was better able to build one than anybody else. He was always anxious to benefit the community as much as possible, and he undertook it. It cost a great deal of money and was a very bad investment. I had the foundation dug and superintended its erection. I have had quantities of letters from him, giving instructions about that mill. He employed a man named Shoemaker, from the North, who was used to building mills, to assist him in planning and building it. It was built of rock. It was a large building, four stories high, and had four run of stone. The dam was three-fourths of a mile above the mill, and a canal was made that distance along the bank of the river, to bring the water to the mill. That dam and canal cost thousands of dollars. Two-thirds of the way the canal was through blue mountain rock—not limestone—that had to be blown out. It had to be nine feet wide, to allow the bateaux to pass through to Charlottesville. It all cost a great deal of money.[1] After the mill was completed and we had commenced making flour, there came a big freshet and swept away the dam. I never felt worse. We had eleven thousand bushels of grain in the mill, and coopers and other hands employed, and I thought we were ruined. But it didn't move him a bit. He never seemed to get tired of paying out money for it. He was always greatly interested in its erection and in carrying it on. All my letters were full of instructions about it. Here are some of them:

MEMORANDUMS FOR MR. BACON

Do the abutment of the dam as soon as the scow is ready, and get the scow made immediately. Then deliver the scow, with a good strong chain of sufficient length, to Mr. Showmaker.

Stop the leak under the bridge just above the waste.

Fill up the stone wanting at the waste.

Strengthen the bank of the canal at the toll mill.

Make the wagon way on the south side of the great mill.

Dig the foundation of the wall in the ground floor of the great mill, whenever Mr. Maddox is ready to do the wall, and level the floor.

Keep the thorns constantly clean wed.

In harvest time send all your hands to assist Mr. Randolph, and let them be with him through his whole harvest, except when wanting to secure our own oats.

Wormly must be directed to weed the flower beds about the house, the nursery, the vineyards, and raspberry beds, when they want it.

I wish him also to gather me a peck or two of clean broom seed, when ripe.

I have bought 3 mules of Mr. Peter Minor in Louisa, which we are to bring home immediately. They are to be broke immediately, but should not be worked more than half their time.

Put the Jenny and our 2 mares to the Jack.

Give wool to any of my negro women who desire it, as well those with Mr. Craven as others, but particularly to the house women here.

I think you should scarcely miss a day visiting the mill, and the top of the mountain also, to see that every thing is right at both places, and particularly that no animals of any kind get into the inclosure at the mountain, or are turned at large into it.

Pay great attention to the hogs and sheep. We must get into such a stock as to have 30 killable hogs every year, and fifty ewes. Col. Coles is to have a ram lamb from us of this year. Let it be the best. He will send for it when weaned.

Use great economy in timber, never cutting down a tree for fire-wood or any other purpose as long as one can be found ready cut down, and tolerably convenient. In our new way of fencing, the shortest cuts and large branches, and even hollow trees, will come in for use. The loppings will do for fire-wood and coal wood.

If a couple more of good mules, two, or rather three years old, can be got for fifty or sixty dollars, at credit of not less than 90 days from the time I am informed of it, I shall be glad to have them bought. I am told very fine may be got, and cheap, in Fluvana, and particularly that a Mr. Quarles has some to sell.

May 13, 1807

Washington, Nov. 9, 1807

Sir,—

I now inclose you $250, of which $100 is for James Walker, $50 for Mr. Maddox, and $100 towards paying such of your debts as are most pressing. Another like remittance the next month will, I hope, begin to place you at your ease. Mr. Peyton sent me an order from Maddox for $50, but at the date of the order you had in hand that sum for him. It will therefore be necessary for you to get Mr. Maddox and Mr. Peyton to agree to which of them this $50 is to be paid. If they do not agree, then it must be paid to Mr. Maddox, as I have not made myself liable for it to Mr. Peyton. I shall be perfectly willing that the waterman to whom you are disposed to sell property should bring up articles for me. I am just now sending off to Richmond 8 trunks of books and 4 other packages, weighing in all about 5,000 weight, as I guess, which will probably be in Richmond in all the last week of this month. They are well secured, but would still require to be as well guarded as possible against rain from above or the water of the boat below. If your boatman will undertake to have special care of them, they will be a good beginning in your account. I tender my best wishes.

Th. Jefferson

Mr. E. Bacon

DIRECTIONS FOR MR. BACON
June 7, 1808

Consider as your first object the keeping a full supply of water to the mill, observing that whenever the water does not run over the waste, you should take your hands, and having put in a sufficiency of stone, then carry in earth and heighten till the water runs steadily over the waste. It ought to do this when both mills are running one pair of stones each. Take Mr. Randolph's advice on these occasions.

You will furnish Mr. Maddox, while working on the stable, with attendance, hauling, lime, and sand, so that I may only have to pay him for laying the stone. I presume Mr. Dinsmore will let him be of his mess while here. If objected to, however, do for him what you can best.

As soon as the sashes are ready for Bedford, furnish Mr. Randolph 3 of your best hands, instead of his waterman, who are to carry the sashes, tables, and other things up to Lynchburg, and to give notice of their arrival to Mr. Chisolm, who will then be in Bedford, and will have Jerry's wagon there, which he must send for the things to Lynchburg. In the mean time, they must be lodged at Mr. Brown's, at Lynchburg.

Jerry is to go to Bedford with his wagon as soon as Mr. Chisolm goes.

At harvest, give your whole force to Mr. Randolph, to assist in his harvest; the nailers, as well as all the rest, except Johnny Hemings and Lewis.

Consider the garden as your main business and push it with all your might when the interruptions permit.

Rake and sweep the charcoal on the level into little heaps, and carry them off. Rather do this when the grass seed is ripe.

I used to sell a good deal of the flour in Richmond. The mill was on the Fluvanna, the north prong of the James River, and I used to send it down on bateaux. I remember sending off at one time three bateau loads—between two hundred and fifty and three hundred barrels—made of new wheat. I started on horseback in time to get to Richmond before the flour. When I told the landlord I had new flour on the way, "Well, sir," said he, "you will be certain to get a good price for it, for there is hardly a barrel in the city." I had notice circulated that a lot of new flour would arrive and be sold at the river at four o'clock. There was a large crowd, and I sold every barrel, at fourteen dollars a barrel, as fast as it could be rolled ashore, and it didn't begin to supply the demand. I got my money from the bank, and started after supper, and rode home that night. It was just sixty-three miles; but I had a fine sorrel mare that Mr. Jefferson appropriated for my use, and I made it easily. As soon as I got home, I went directly to Mr. Jefferson's room with the money. I remember it distinctly. It was the first money of the old United States Bank I had ever seen. The bills were new out of the bank and very pretty. Mr. Jefferson, as you know, was always very strongly opposed to the United States Bank. As I paid it over to him, I remarked that it was very handsome money. "Yes, sir," said he, "and very convenient, if people would only use it properly. But they will not. It will lead to speculation, inflation, and trouble."

Mr. Jefferson had a nail factory a good many years, which was a great convenience to the people and very profitable. He worked ten hands in it, had two fires, and five hands at a fire. These hands could clear two dollars a day, besides paying for the coal and iron rods. After the embargo and the War of 1812, we could not get rods and were obliged to give it up. We supplied the stores all over that country with nails and sold a great many to the people to build their houses. I sold Mr. Monroe the nails to build his house.[2]

Mr. Jefferson also had a factory for making domestic cloth. He got his cotton from Richmond in bateaux. He had in his factory three spinning machines. One had thirty-six spindles, one eighteen, and one six. The hands used to learn on the little one. He made cloth for all his servants and a great deal besides. I have sold wagon loads of it to the merchants.[3]

He had a good blacksmith shop. A man named Stewart was at the head of that. He was a fine workman, but he would have his sprees—would get drunk. Mr. Jefferson kept him a good many years longer than he would have done because he wanted him to teach some of his own hands.[4]

Dinsmore, who lived with him a good many years, was the most ingenious hand to work with wood I ever knew. He could make anything. He made a great deal of nice mahogany furniture, helped make the carriage, worked on the University, and could do any kind of fine work that was wanted. Burwell was a fine painter. With all these he could have almost anything that he needed made on his own plantation.[5]

VI

Mr. Jefferson's Personal Appearance and Habits

MR. JEFFERSON was six feet two and a half inches high, well proportioned, and straight as a gun barrel. He was like a fine horse; he had no surplus flesh. He had an iron constitution and was very strong.[1] He had a machine for measuring strength. There were very few men that I have seen try it that were as strong in the arms as his son-in-law, Colonel Thomas Mann Randolph; but Mr. Jefferson was stronger than he.[2] He always enjoyed the best of health. I don't think he was ever really sick until his last sickness.[3] His skin was very clear and pure—just like he was in principle. He had blue eyes. His countenance was always mild and pleasant. You never saw it ruffled. No odds what happened, it always maintained the same expression. When I was sometimes very much fretted and disturbed, his countenance was perfectly unmoved. I remember one case in particular. We had about eleven thousand bushels of wheat in the mill, and coopers and everything else employed. There was a big freshet—the first after the dam was finished. It was raining powerfully. I got up early in the morning and went up to the dam. While I stood there, it began to break, and I stood and saw the freshet sweep it all away. I never felt worse. I did not know what we should do. I went up to see Mr. Jefferson. He had just come from breakfast. "Well, sir," said he, "have you heard from the river?" I said,

"Yes, sir; I have just come from there with very bad news. The milldam is all swept away." "Well, sir," said he, just as calm and quiet as though nothing had happened, "we can't make a new dam this summer, but we will get Lewis' ferryboat, with our own, and get the hands from all the quarters, and boat in rock enough in place of the dam to answer for the present and next summer. I will send to Baltimore and get ship bolts, and we will make a dam that the freshet can't wash away." He then went on and explained to me in detail just how he would have the dam built. We repaired the dam as he suggested, and the next summer we made a new dam that I reckon must be there yet.[4]

Mr. Jefferson was always an early riser—arose at daybreak or before. The sun never found him in bed. I used sometimes to think, when I went up there *very* early in the morning, that I would find him in bed; but there he would be before me, walking on the terrace.[5]

He never had a servant make a fire in his room in the morning, or at any other time, when he was at home. He always had a box filled with nice dry wood in his room, and when he wanted fire he would open it and put on the wood. He would always have a good many ashes in his fireplace, and when he went out he would cover up his fire very carefully, and when he came back he would uncover the coals and make a fire for himself.

He did not use tobacco in any form. He never used a profane word or anything like it. He never played cards. I never saw a card in the house at Monticello, and I had particular orders from him to suppress card-playing among the Negroes, who, you know, are generally very fond of it. I never saw any dancing in his house, and if there had been any there during the twenty years I was with him I should certainly have known it.[6] He was never a great eater, but what he did eat he wanted to be very choice. He never eat much hog meat. He often told me, as I was giving out meat for the servants, that what I gave one of them for a week would be more than he would use in six months.[7] When he was coming home from Washington, I generally knew it, and got ready for him, and waited at the house to give him the keys. After saying, "How are all?" and talking awhile, he would say, "What have you got that is good?" I knew mighty well what suited him. He was especially fond of Guinea fowls; and for meat he preferred good beef, mutton, and lambs. Those broad-tailed sheep I told you about made the finest mutton I ever saw. Meriwether Lewis' mother made very nice hams, and every year I used to get a few from her for his special use. He was very fond of vegetables and fruit and raised every variety of them. He was very ingenious. He invented a plough that was considered a great improvement on any that had ever been used. He got a great many premiums and medals for it.[8] He planned his own carriage, buildings, garden, fences, and a good many other things. He was nearly always busy upon some plan or model.

Every day, just as regularly as the day came, unless the weather was very bad, he would have his horse brought out and take his ride. The boy who took care of his horse knew what time he started, and would bring him out for him, and hitch him in his place. He generally started about nine o'clock. He was an uncommonly fine rider—sat easily upon his horse and always had him in the most perfect control. After he returned from Washington he generally rode Brimmer or Tecumseh until I bought Eagle for him of Captain John Graves, of Louisa County, just before I left him.

He was always very neat in his dress, wore short breeches and bright shoe buckles. When he rode on horseback he had a pair of overalls that he always put on.[9]

Mr. Jefferson never debarred himself from hearing any preacher that came along. There was a Mr. Hiter, a Baptist preacher, that used to preach occasionally at the Charlottesville Courthouse. He had no regular church but was a kind of missionary—rode all over the country and preached. He wasn't much of a preacher, was uneducated, but he was a good man. Everybody had confidence in him, and they went to hear him on that account. Mr. Jefferson's nephews Peter Carr, Sam Carr, and Dabney Carr thought a great deal of him. I have often heard them talk about him. Mr. Jefferson nearly always went to hear him when he came around. I remember his being there one day in particular. His servant came with him and brought a seat—a kind of campstool—upon which he sat. After Mr. Jefferson got old and feeble, a servant used to go with him over the plantation and carry that stool, so that he could sit down while he was waiting and attending to any kind of work that was going on. After the sermon there was a proposition to pass around the hat and raise money to buy the preacher a horse. Mr. Jefferson did not wait for the hat. I saw him unbutton his overalls, and get his hand into his pocket, and take out a handful of silver, I don't know how much. He then walked across the Courthouse to Mr. Hiter and gave it into his hand. He bowed very politely to Mr. Jefferson and seemed to be very much pleased.

Mr. Jefferson was very liberal and kind to the poor. When he would come from Washington, the poor people all about the country would find it out immediately and would come in crowds to Monticello to beg him. He would give them notes to me directing me what to give them.[10] I knew them all a great deal better than he did. Many of them I knew were not worthy — were just lazy, good-for-nothing people, and I would not give them anything. When I saw Mr. Jefferson, I told him who they were and that he ought not to encourage them in their laziness. He told me that when they came to him and told him their pitiful tales, he could not refuse them, and he did not know what to do. I told him to send them to me. He did so, but they never would come. They knew what to expect.

In, I think, the year 1816, there was a very severe frost, and the corn was almost destroyed. It was so badly injured that it would hardly make bread, and it was thought that the stock was injured by eating it. There was a neighborhood at the base of the Blue Ridge where the frost did not injure the corn. They had a good crop, and the people were obliged to give them just what they were disposed to ask for it. I went up there and bought thirty barrels for Mr. Jefferson of a Mr. Massey—gave him ten dollars a barrel for it. That spring the poor trifling people came in crowds for corn. I sent the wagon after what I had bought, and by the time it would get back Mr. Jefferson had given out so many of his little orders that it would pretty much take the load. I could hardly get it hauled as fast as he would give it away. I went to Mr. Jefferson and told him it never would do; we could not give ten dollars a barrel for corn, and haul it thirty miles, and give it away after that fashion. He said, "What can I do? These people tell me they have no corn, and it will not do to let them suffer." I told him again, I could tell him what to do. Just send them all to me. I knew them all a great deal better than he did and would give to all that were really deserving.

There was an old woman named — who used to trouble us a great deal. She had three daughters that were bad girls—large, strapping, lazy things—and the old woman would beg for them. One day she went to Mr. Jefferson in a mean old dress, and told him some pitiful story, and he gave her a note to me directing me to give her two bushels of meal. I did so. The same day she went to Mrs. Randolph and got three sides of bacon—middling meat. There was more than she could carry and she had two of her daughters' illegitimate children to help her carry it home. When she got to the river, the old Negro who attended the ferry was so mad to see her carrying off the meat that he would not ferry her over. So she laid the meat on the edge of the boat, and they ferried themselves across. When the boat struck the bank it jarred the meat off, and it went to the bottom of the river, and she had a great deal of trouble to get it.

Afterwards she went to Mr. Jefferson and told him the meal I gave her was not good—would not make bread—and he sent her to me again. I told her the meal in the mill was all alike, and she could only get better by going to the Blue Ridge for corn. She said she had no horse, it was too far to walk, and she could not go. I told her I would furnish her a mule. Mr. Jefferson had an old mule that must have been thirty or forty years old, called Dolphin.[11] He was too old to work and we did not like to kill him. His hair grew very long, and he was a sight to look at. He was too old to jump much, but he would tear down the fence with his nose and go over the plantation pretty much as he pleased. I was very anxious to get rid of the mule and of the old woman too, and I thought that maybe if I loaned her the mule she would not come back. So I told her she could have the old mule and go get her corn. She came and stayed overnight, so as to get an early start. My wife gave her a coffee sack, and I gave her an order on Massey, and she started off on old Dolphin. When she got up there the people knew nothing about her, and she could do so much better begging, that, sure enough, she never came back at all. Mr. Jefferson used to enjoy telling people how I got rid of the old woman and Dolphin. She soon sent for her daughters. Two of them went up there; but a man named — — had taken up with one of them, and he moved her off into another neighborhood. He was a well-educated man, and much of a gentleman. His poor old mother was a mighty good woman, and she was so distressed about it that it almost made her crazy.

Some six weeks or two months after the old woman had gone, I saw something moving about in the wheat field, and, sure enough, there was Dolphin home again. After this there was a couple of Kentucky drovers named Scott and Dudley, from whom we used to buy a good many mules for the plantation, came along with a drove. I told them about the trouble we had with Dolphin. They said they would take him away so that he would trouble us no more, and I gave him to them. They sheared off his long hair and trimmed him up so that he looked quite well. They found one in the drove that matched him very well, and went on a few miles, and sold the pair to Hon. Hugh Nelson. He was a Congressman. He and William C. Rives married sisters, daughters of Frank Walker.[12] He was very wealthy and popular. I knew his father, too, Colonel Walker. He used to wear short breeches and shoe buckles. It wasn't long before Dolphin was back, and I told Mr. Jefferson. He laughed and said, "You treat him so much better than anybody else will, that he will come back and see you." When Mr. Nelson's overseer came over for him I asked him how old he supposed he was. He said he could not tell. I then told him his history. He took him off, and we never saw any more of Dolphin.

Mr. Jefferson was very particular in the transaction of all his business. He kept an account of everything. Nothing was too small for him to keep an account of. He knew exactly how much of everything was raised at each plantation, and what became of it; how much was sold, and how much fed out. Here is one of his little crop accounts. All the overseers had such. Some of them used to grumble over them mightily. But I told them we were paid by Mr. Jefferson to attend to his business, and we ought to do it exactly as he wanted it done. One of them to whom I gave one of these little papers one day, after fretting a good deal about it, said,

ESTIMATE OF GRAIN
From Oct. 1, 1819, to July 7, 1820, 40 weeks

	Bar.
90 persons from Oct. 1 to July 7.20, 40 weeks, @ 4½ b. a week,	180
70 hogs to be fattened, @ 1½ bar. a piece,	105
9 breeding sows @ 1 pint a day, from Dec. 1 to Mar. 10, 100 days,	3
60 shoats @ ½ pint a day, 100 days,	9½
pigs	5
6 beeves @ 2 gal. a day, from Dec. 1 to Mar. 1 (killing off) say 90 days	27
Stable @ 14 gals. a day, Oct. 1 to July 1 (deducting 2 mo.) 210 days,	73½
1 plantation horse and 6 mules, @ 1½ bush. a day, Oct. 1 to July 1, 270 d.,	81
Sheep, suppose 80, @ ½ pint from Dec. 1 to Mar. 15, 90 d.,	11
4 oxen @ 6 galls. a day, Dec. 1 to May 15, 165 d.,	25
1 milch cow at the stable, @ 1 peck a day, 165 d.,	8
The other cattle to be fed on stalks, tops, shucks, chaff, straw, &c.	
	528

RESOURCES			Bar.
Oct. 1, corn on hand in the mill,......................			80
from Th. J. R.................................			200
Mill @ 2 bar, a week, 40 weeks,......................			80
	lb.	b.	
Offal of 350 b. flour, @ 25		35	
Do. to be bought at mill,		65	100
			460
340 lbs. to be bought elsewhere,......................			68
			528

"Well, I believe if Mr. Jefferson told you to go into the fire, you would follow his instructions."

I reported to Mr. Jefferson every dollar that I received and just what I paid it out for. The first day of every January I gave him a full list of all the servants, stock, and everything on the place, so that he could see exactly what had been the gain or loss. In all his business transactions with people, he had everything put down in writing, so that there was no chance for any misunderstanding. There was quite a village at Milton. It was the head of navigation for bateaux. A great deal of flour, grain, and other produce was brought from the western part of the state and shipped there, the wagons carrying back groceries and other things that the bateaux had brought from Richmond. This and other business employed a good many families. Nearly all the families in Milton were supplied with firewood from Mr. Jefferson's estate. They paid him five dollars a year for what wood they would burn in a fireplace. Mr. Jefferson wrote a blank form for me, and I made a written contract with all the people who got their firewood from his place, and once a year I went around and made collections. Here is the blank form that he wrote for me that I filled out, and from which I copied all these contracts for wood:

These presents witness that the subscriber, Thomas Jefferson, has leased to the subscriber, James Marr, of the town of Milton, a right, in common with other lessees, to cut and take away sufficient firewood for one fireplace from the lands of the said Thomas Jefferson, on the south side of the road leading through Milton towards Colle, for the year which began on the 1st day of October last past, and ending the 1st day of October of the present year, 1813; the said James Marr yielding and paying to the said Thomas Jefferson five dollars on the 1st day of October closing the year, which he covenants to do, and it is further agreed that this lease, and on the same conditions, shall continue from year to year until notice to the contrary be given by either party to the other. Witness their hands this 6th day of February, 1813.

TH. JEFFERSON

Witness,   JAMES MARR
E. Bacon[13]

He was just as particular as this with all his business. Whenever I engaged an overseer for him, or any kind of a mechanic, I always made a written contract with him that stated just what he was to do and just what pay he was to receive. In this way he avoided all difficulties with the men he employed. I used to write Mr. Jefferson's name so often to contracts that I made for him that I could imitate his signature almost exactly. A good many people could not tell whether he or I had written his name.[14] Here is one of my contracts with a carpenter, written and signed by myself for **Mr.** Jefferson:

It is agreed between Thomas Jefferson and Richard Durrett, both of the county of Albemarle, that the said Durrett shall serve the said Jefferson one year as a carpenter.[15] And the said Durrett does by these presents oblige himself to do whatever work the said Jefferson shall require in the business of carpenter's work; and the said Durrett obliges himself to faithfully do his duty. The year commences on the day that the said Durrett shall take charge of the said Jefferson's employ; for which year's service the said Jefferson agrees to pay the said Durrett forty pounds, and to find him four hundred and fifty pounds of pork, and a peck of corn meal a week; or, in case the said Durrett should have three in family, the said Jefferson agrees to find him three pecks a week, and to find him a cow to give milk from 15th April to 15th November. As witness our hands this 28th of October, 1812.

RICHARD DURRETT
E. BACON, for
TH. JEFFERSON

VII

Mr. Jefferson's Family

MR. JEFFERSON had four children. Two of them died very young. The other two, Martha and Maria, were in France with him while he was Minister. They were in school there. Martha married Colonel Thomas Mann Randolph, afterwards governor of Virginia. Maria married John W. Eppes. He afterwards went to Congress. He was a very fine-looking man and a great favorite with everybody. Mrs. Eppes died very young and was buried at Monticello. She had one boy, Frank Eppes, a fine little fellow. He used to stay at Monticello a good deal.[1]

I knew Mrs. Randolph as well as I ever knew any person out of my own family. Few such women ever lived. I never saw her equal. I was with Mr. Jefferson twenty years and saw her frequently every week. I never saw her at all out of temper. I can truly say that I never saw two such persons in this respect as she and her father. Sometimes he would refer me to her, or she would refer me to him, a half dozen times in a day. Mrs. Randolph was more like her father than any lady I ever saw. She was nearly as tall as he, and had the same clear, bright complexion and blue eyes. I have rode over the plantation, I reckon, a thousand times with Mr. Jefferson, and when he was not talking he was nearly always humming some tune, or singing in a low tone to himself.[2] And it was just so with Mrs.

Randolph. As she was attending to her duties about the house, she seemed to be always in a happy mood. She had always her father's pleasant smile and was nearly always humming some tune. I have never seen her at all disturbed by any amount of care and trouble.

Mr. Jefferson was the most industrious person I ever saw in my life. All the time I was with him I had full permission to visit his room whenever I thought it necessary to see him on any business. I knew how to get into his room at any time of day or night. I have sometimes gone into his room when he was in bed, but aside from that I never went into it but twice in the whole twenty years I was with him that I did not find him employed. I never saw him sitting idle in his room but twice. Once he was suffering with the toothache; and once, in returning from his Bedford farm, he had slept in a room where some of the glass had been broken out of the window, and the wind had blown upon him and given him a kind of neuralgia. At all other times he was either reading, writing, talking, working upon some model, or doing something else.[3]

Mrs. Randolph was just like her father in this respect. She was always busy. If she wasn't reading or writing, she was always doing something. She used to sit in Mr. Jefferson's room a great deal and sew, or read, or talk, as he would be busy about something else. As her daughters grew up, she taught them to be industrious like herself.[4] They used to take turns each day in giving out to the servants and superintending the housekeeping. I knew all her children just as well as I did my own. There were six daughters and five sons. Let me see if I can remember their names. The boys were Thomas Jefferson, James Madison, Benjamin Franklin, Meriwether Lewis, and George Wythe. The daughters were Anne, Ellen, Virginia, Cornelia, and a little thing that could just run about when I came away. Her name was Septimis, or something like that.* Only two of them were married when I came away. Jeff married Jane Nicholas, daughter of Governor Wilson C. Nicholas, and Anne married Charles S. Bankhead. Anne, Ellen, and Meriwether Lewis had the fresh rosy countenance of the Jefferson family. The rest of the family, as far as I can remember—I don't remember about the little ones—had the Randolph complexion, which was dark and Indianlike. You know they claim to be descended from Pocahontas. Virginia and Cornelia were tall, active, and fine-looking, with very dark complexions.[5]

Mr. Jefferson was perfectly devoted to his grandchildren, and they to him. They delighted to follow him about over the grounds and garden, and he took great pleasure in talking with them, and giving them advice, and directing their sports. I have heard him tell them enough of times that nobody should live without some useful employment. I always raised my boys to work. Mr. Jefferson knew this, and it pleased him. On Saturdays, when they were not in school, they often cut coal wood for the nailery. They could cut a cord a day and earn fifty cents. Governor Randolph once told them that if they would cut off the bushes from a certain field, he would give them twenty dollars. His boys

* Septimia. [Pierson's note.]

would often go and work with them like little Turks on Saturdays, so that my boys could go with them a-fishing. After a while they finished their job and got their pay. Mr. Jefferson heard of it. One evening I heard him talking with his grandchildren about it. He told them my boys had got twenty dollars—more money than any of them had got; that they had earned it themselves, and said a great deal in their praise and in regard to the importance of industrious habits. Meriwether Lewis was a very bright little fellow. I always thought him the most sprightly of all the Randolph children. He spoke up and said, "Why, grandpa, if we should work like Fielding and Thomas, our hands would get so rough and sore that we could not hold our books. And we need not work so. We shall be rich, and all we want is a good education, so that we shall be prepared to associate with wealthy and intelligent people." "Ah!" said Mr. Jefferson, and I have thought of the remark a thousand times since, "those that expect to get through the world without industry, because they are rich, will be greatly mistaken. The people that *do* work will soon get possession of all their property." I have heard him give those children a great deal of good advice. I remember, once, hearing him tell them that they should never laugh in a loud, boisterous manner in company or in the presence of strangers. That was his own habit.

He took great pleasure in the sports and plays of his grandchildren. I have often seen him direct them and enjoy them greatly. The large lawn back of the house was a fine place for their plays. They very often ran races, and he would give the word for them to start and decide who was the winner. Another play was stealing goods. They would divide into two parties and lay down their coats, hats, knives, and other things, and each party would try to get all that the other had. If they were caught in the attempt to steal, they were made prisoners. I have seen Mr. Jefferson laugh heartily to see this play go on. The children about the country used to enjoy coming there. It was a fine place for them to play, and in the fruit season there was always the greatest quantities of good fruit. Jeff Randolph used very often to bring his schoolmates there.[6]

Before the University of Virginia was established, a man of the name of Oglesby taught a school at Charlottesville. I think he was a Scotchman. I know he was a foreigner. He was a fine teacher and had a very large school. Thomas Jefferson Randolph, William C. Rives, Walker Gilmer, Vaul W. Southall, William F. Gordon, and a host of other boys went to his school. Almost every Friday evening Jeff Randolph would bring a lot of his mates to Monticello to play and eat fruit. If they did not come on Friday, they were pretty certain to come on Saturday. I gave them the keys of the house and garden, and very often they all stayed there overnight. One Saturday a lot of the schoolboys that were not invited concluded that they would come also and help themselves to fruit. They went around the back side of the garden, broke off the palings, and got in. They then climbed the trees and broke off a good many limbs, and did a great deal of damage. The other party attacked them, and they had a tremendous fight. The party that had broken in was much the largest, and they could not drive them off. They threw stones at the old gardener and hurt him very badly. They sent to the mill for me, and when I got there the other party were gone, and some of Jeff's party were a good deal hurt. Vaul Southall was very bloody. He had fought like a little tiger. William C. Rives was one of Jeff's party. He was an uncommonly fine boy and was always the peacemaker among the boys. Whenever they got into a difficulty among themselves, they would all say, "Let Willie Rives settle it." Both parties were always willing to select him as umpire. So I said to him, "Willie, why didn't you settle this matter without all this fighting?" He was very much excited, as well as all the rest of them. "Why, sir," said he, "you know that I am a little fellow and couldn't do much fighting, but I called them all the hard names I could think of, and then I started to turn Rompo loose on them, and they all ran off." Rompo was a very fierce dog. I should like very much to see William C. Rives now. I suppose he is quite an old man, though I was a man grown when he was a little boy. He was at Monticello a great deal. Very often he did not like the doings of the other boys, when I gave them the keys to stay up there alone, and he would come down and stay all night at my house. He has stayed there many a night. The other boys were too intimate with the Negro women to suit him. He was always a very modest boy.[7] I once heard one of the other boys make a vulgar remark. He said, "Such talk as that ought not to be thought, much less spoken out." Mr. Jefferson thought a great deal of him, and so did all the family. I think it would have suited them all mighty well if he had married Ellen. But I don't think he ever courted her, and I don't know that she would have married him if he had. He got in love with Miss Walker and married her. I remember Ellen was one day at my house, and my wife was joking her about him, telling her what a fine thing it would be, he was such a fine young man and had such a large property. After a while she said, "Oh, he is too much of a runt to make anybody a husband," and ran off as fast as she could.

Governor Randolph, Mr. Jefferson's son-in-law, was a very eccentric man and would often do the most strange and laughable things.[8] I remember, once, going with him to Edgehill, his plantation, to look after the hands that were at work in the harvest field, cutting and putting up the wheat. He looked at the shocks, and a good many of them were not put up to suit him. He was riding Dromedary. Suddenly he dashed away and rode him right through a large number of the shocks, scattering them in all directions. We then rode on to where the overseer was engaged with the hands. After getting through with all his business with the overseer, as he was leaving he told him he thought the old bull must have been in the lot; he had seen a good many shocks torn down and scattered about as he came along. The overseer looked at me and laughed. He understood the matter perfectly.

The main road from the western part of the state to Richmond ran between Monticello and Edgehill. There was always a great deal of hauling on that road, and teams were almost constantly passing. They got in the habit of camping in the lane just beyond Mr. Randolph's house, and burnt his rails, and made him a heap of trouble. He sent his overseer one night to remonstrate with them against burning his rails. There were a large number of them, and they just laughed at him and finally gave him a tremendous whipping. When Mr. Randolph heard of it he said he would go himself next time. He was tall, swarthy, and raw-boned—one of the stoutest men I ever saw—and afraid of nothing. He was generally dressed in the most indifferent manner and was very queer anyway. The Randolphs were all strange people. John Randolph, you know, was one of the most eccentric men that ever lived, and I think Governor Randolph was full out as strange a man as he. They were as much alike as any two steers you ever saw.

A few nights after the overseer was whipped, they camped again, built their fires, were cooking their supper, and Governor Randolph went down to see them. They soon discovered him, creeping about very slyly and watching them, and thought it was somebody trying to steal their horses and ride them off, and they would have a great deal of trouble to find them in the morning. At length they gave chase, and he allowed himself to be very easily taken. They accused him of trying to steal their horses, said they would have him punished, and demanded that he should tell them where a magistrate lived. He pointed to his own house and told them that a magistrate lived there. Two of them led him to it. It was the strangest-looking house you ever saw, as strange as himself. They led him into the piazza, and he told them he would go in and get the magistrate. He soon reappeared with his pistols, let them know he had brought them to his own house, stormed at them with his big grum voice in the roughest manner until he had scared them sufficiently, and then very calmly told them to be careful whom they arrested hereafter, gave them some good advice, and sent them away. I knew one of those wagoners very well. He used often to tell of it and laugh at the way they were taken in by the Governor.

Governor Randolph was a very hard rider. It was a very common thing with him when he was Governor to start from Richmond after supper and ride Dromedary home by daylight next morning. He would do strange things with that horse. They were just suited to each other. I have often seen him take hold of his tail and run him up the mountain as hard as he could go.

Mr. Jefferson, Mr. Randolph, and I were once riding up the mountain together, and we overtook an old bald-headed Negro, who did nothing but haul wood and water. "Isaac," said Mr. Randolph, with his big grum voice, "have you got any tobacco?" "Yes, master," said he, taking off his hat and making a low bow with a great flourish, and handed him the tobacco out of the top of his hat. Mr. Jefferson laughed and said, "It comes from a very shining place."

Governor Randolph was a very poor manager. He often had to sell off Negroes to pay his debts. Here is a bill of sale for a woman I bought of him. She belonged to an excellent family of servants. He wished me to take another woman instead of her, but I preferred her decidedly and would not do it, and, as he was obliged to raise the money, he let me have her.

BILL OF SALE

I hereby convey to Edmund Bacon, for the sum of five hundred dollars, namely, in cash five hundred dollars, and in his note of hand $ due on demand, a full and indefeasible right, title, and estate in a female slave, Maria, daughter of Iris, born at Edgehill, this day put into his possession, and I, for myself, my heirs, executors, administrators, &c., the said title to the said slave do forever warrant and defend to the said Bacon, his heirs or assigns. Witness my hand and seal this October 9th, 1818.

TH. M. RANDOLPH [Seal.]

Done in presence of
   Daniel Caldase
   William F. Cardin
   James O. Wallers

While he was Governor his debts troubled him a great deal. I often loaned him money, and he often applied to me to help him raise it from others. When he must have it and could get it in no other way, he would be obliged to sell some of his Negroes. Here is one of his letters to me.

It is superscribed:

Mr. EDM. BACON, BY PHIL

Dear Sir: It is so absolutely necessary to me to have as much as $150 by to-morrow evening, to send by express to pay into the Bank of U. S., and Bank of Virginia in Richmond, before 3 o'clock on Wednesday next, that I am forced, against my will, to importune you farther with the offer of the little girl at Edgehill. Do you think it would be possible for us to borrow that money between us by 3 o'clock to-morrow? I should have set off down to-day, but the hope of succeeding to-morrow so as to do by sending, has stopped me. I am obliged to be in Richmond on the Board of Public Works week after next, and my presence is more wanted now at Edgehill than Varina. Besides my wife is really ill to-day. Could you prevail on your mother to lend as much money?

Your friend,
TH. M. RANDOLPH

Mr. Bacon   May 9, 1819

I raised the money for him and the next day paid him two hundred dollars for Edy. She was a little girl four years old. He gave me this receipt:

Received from Edmund Bacon two hundred dollars for Edy, daughter of Fennel, now at Edgehill, and I bind myself to make a complete title in the said Edy to the said Bacon. Witness my hand, this May 16, 1819.

TH. M. RANDOLPH

He was finally unable to meet his obligations, failed completely, and lost everything. Mr. Jefferson, in making his will,* had to take especial care to prevent Mr. Randolph's creditors from getting what property he left for Mrs. Randolph.

Before he died his mind became shattered, and he pretty much lost his reason. He had no control of his

---

* See Mr. Jefferson's will in the Appendix. [Pierson's note.]

temper. I have seen him cane his son Jeff after he was a grown man. Jeff made no resistance, but got away from him as soon as he could.[9] I have seen him knock down his son-in-law Charles L. Bankhead with an iron poker. Bankhead married his daughter Anne. She was a perfectly lovely woman. She was a Jefferson in temper. He was the son of a very wealthy man who lived near Fredericksburg. He was a fine-looking man, but a terrible drunkard. I have seen him ride his horse into the barroom at Charlottesville and get a drink of liquor. I have seen his wife run from him when he was drunk and hide in a potato hole to get out of danger. He once stabbed Jeff Randolph because he had said something about his abuse of his sister, and I think would have killed him, if I had not interfered and separated them.[10]

One night he was very drunk and made a great disturbance, because Burwell, who kept the keys, would not give him any more brandy. Mrs. Randolph could not manage him, and she sent for me. She would never call on Mr. Randolph at such a time, he was so excitable. But he heard the noise in the dining room and rushed in to see what was the matter. He entered the room just as I did, and Bankhead, thinking he was Burwell, began to curse him. Seizing an iron poker that was standing by the fireplace, he knocked him down as quick as I ever saw a bullock fall. The blow pealed the skin off one side of his forehead and face, and he bled terribly. If it had been a square blow, instead of glancing off as it did, it must have killed him.

Bankhead came to me one court day at Charlottesville and told me he did not want me and one of our
overseers that was with me to leave him that day. He
did not tell us what he wanted, and we had no idea. We
saw that he did not get drunk that day as usual, and we
were surprised at that. Towards night he came to us
and said he wanted us to start home with him. We rode
out of town some distance towards Monticello, and he
got off his horse and hitched him to the fence, and
requested us to hitch ours and stay with him. We still
had no idea of what he was about, or what he wanted of
us. At length Phil Barbour and William F. Gordon
rode along. Gordon had been employed in a suit
against Bankhead, and in making his speech he had
taken a lawyer's privilege and said a good many severe
things about him, for which he had determined to fight
him. Bankhead went out immediately in front of
Gordon and requested him to get down; said he
wanted to speak to him. Gordon made some excuse and
declined. Bankhead asked him again, and Gordon, who
seemed to have no idea what he wanted, gave some
reason that I have forgotten and again declined. Bankhead then told him he had insulted him and began to
curse him with all his might. He told him that he was
armed, and that if he did not get down, he would bring
him down—he would shoot him; "but," said he, "if you
will get down, I will throw away my pistols and agree
to fight you with nothing but what my mother gave
me." It was no use for Gordon to refuse, nor for us to
try to prevent the fight. He got off his horse, and he
had hardly touched the ground, before at it they went,

and I never in all my life saw such a fight. They fought and fought, and neither seemed to get the least bit of advantage over the other. They clinched several times, and tried to throw each other down, but both were strong and supple. Neither could get the other down. I never did see as even a match. I think they must have fought a half an hour, and both of them were as bloody as butchers, when I told Phil Barbour it would never do for us to let them fight any longer—we must separate them. So he took hold of Gordon, and I took hold of Bankhead, and we just pulled them apart.

Bankhead got the worst of it. One eye was badly injured, and I think never did get entirely over the hurt. Bankhead was the stoutest, but Gordon had the best wind. I often heard him describe the fight and laugh about it afterwards. He said he thought of crying "Enough!" several times, but Bankhead kept him so busy he hadn't time.

I bought a Negro woman and her two children of Bankhead. Here is his receipt:

This writing proves that I have sold and received payment for a negro woman named Winny, and her two children, and that I promise and am bound to give a bill of sale for s'd negro's, having received payment. As witness my hand, &c.

CHAS. L. BANKHEAD

Test,
  Thos. Wells
1st July, 1814

VIII

Mr. Jefferson's Servants

MR. JEFFERSON was always very kind and indulgent to his servants.[1] He would not allow them to be at all overworked, and he would hardly ever allow one of them to be whipped. His orders to me were constant: that if there was any servant that could not be got along without the chastising that was customary, to dispose of him. He could not bear to have a servant whipped, no odds how much he deserved it.[2] I remember one case in particular. Mr. Jefferson gave written instructions that I should always sell the nails that were made in his nailery. We made from sixpenny to twentypenny nails and always kept a supply of each kind on hand. I went one day to supply an order, and the eightpenny nails were all gone, and there was a full supply of all the other sizes. Of course they had been stolen. I soon became satisfied that Jim Hubbard, one of the servants that worked in the nailery, had stolen them and charged him with it. He denied it powerfully. I talked with Grady, the overseer of the nailery, about it, and finally I said, "Let us drop it. He has hid them somewhere, and if we say no more about it, we shall find them." I examined his house and every place I could think of, but for some time I could find nothing of the nails. One day after a rain, as I was following a path through the woods, I saw muddy tracks on the leaves leading off from the path. I followed them until

I came to a treetop, where I found the nails buried in a large box. There were several hundred pounds of them. From circumstances I knew that Jim had stolen them. Mr. Jefferson was at home at the time, and when I went up to Monticello I told him of it. He was very much surprised and felt very badly about it. Jim had always been a favorite servant. He told me to be at my house next morning when he took his ride, and he would see Jim there. When he came, I sent for Jim, and I never saw any person, white or black, feel as badly as he did when he saw his master. He was mortified and distressed beyond measure. He had been brought up in the shop, and we all had confidence in him. Now his character was gone. The tears streamed down his face, and he begged pardon over and over again. I felt very badly myself. Mr. Jefferson turned to me, and said, "Ah, sir, we can't punish him. He has suffered enough already." He then talked to him, gave him a heap of good advice, and sent him to the shop. Grady had waited, expecting to be sent for to whip him, and he was astonished to see him come back and go to work after such a crime. When he came to dinner—he boarded with me then—he told me that when Jim came back to the shop, he said, "Well, I'se been a-seeking religion a long time, but I never heard anything before that sounded so, or made me feel so, as I did when master said, 'Go, and don't do so any more'; and now I'se determined to seek religion till I find it"; and sure enough, he afterwards came to me for a permit to go and be baptized. I gave him one and never knew of his doing anything of the sort again. He was always a good servant afterwards.[3]

Mr. Jefferson had a large number of favorite servants that were treated just as well as could be. Burwell was the main, principal servant on the place. He did not go to Washington. Mr. Jefferson had the most perfect confidence in him. He told me not to be at all particular with him—to let him do pretty much as he pleased, and to let him have pocket money occasionally, as he wanted it.

Once or twice every week while Mr. Jefferson was President, I opened every room in the house and had it thoroughly aired. When I was so busy that I could not attend to this myself, I would send the keys to Burwell, and he would air the house, and was, if possible, more particular than I was. He stayed at Monticello and took charge of the meat house, garden, &c., and kept the premises in order. Mr. Jefferson gave him his freedom in his will, and it was right that he should do it.[4]

The house servants were Betty Brown, Sally, Critta, and Betty Hemings, Nance, and Ursula.[5] They were old family servants and great favorites. They were in the room when Mrs. Jefferson died. She died before I went to live with him, and left four little children. He never married again. They have often told my wife that when Mrs. Jefferson died they stood around the bed. Mr. Jefferson sat by her, and she gave him directions about a good many things that she wanted done. When she came to the children, she wept and could not speak for some time. Finally she held up her hand, and spreading out her four fingers, she told him she could not die happy if she thought her four children were ever to have a stepmother brought in over them. Holding her other hand in his, Mr. Jefferson promised her solemnly that he would never marry again. And he never did. He was then quite a young man and very handsome, and I suppose he could have married well; but he always kept that promise.[6]

These women remained at Monticello while he was President. I was instructed to take no control of them. They had very little to do. When I opened the house, they attended to airing it. Then every March we had to bottle all his cider. Dear me, this was a job. It took us two weeks. Mr. Jefferson was very particular about his cider.[7] He gave me instructions to have every apple cleaned perfectly clean when it was made. Here are his instructions:

We have saved red Hughes enough from the north orchard to make a smart cask of cyder. They are now mellow, and beginning to rot. I will pray you, therefore, to have them made into cyder immediately. Let them be made clean one by one, and all the rotten ones thrown away, or the rot cut out. Nothing else can ensure good cyder.

Sally Hemings went to France with Maria Jefferson when she was a little girl. Mr. Jefferson was Minister to France, and he wanted to put her in school there. They crossed the ocean alone. I have often heard her tell about it. When they got to London, they stayed with Mr. Adams, who was Minister there, until Mr. Jefferson came or sent for them. I have read a beautiful letter that Mrs. Adams wrote to her sister, Mrs. Cranch, about her. Here it is:

I have had with me for a fortnight a little daughter of Mr. Jefferson's, who arrived here with a young negro girl, her servant, from Virginia. Mr. Jefferson wrote me some months ago that he expected them, and desired me to receive them. I did so, and was amply repaid for my trouble. A finer child of her age I never saw. So mature and understanding, so womanly a behavior, and so much sensibility, united, are rarely to be met with. I grew so fond of her, and she was so attached to me, that, when Mr. Jefferson sent for her, they were obliged to force the little creature away. She is but eight years old. She would sit, sometimes, and describe to me the parting with her aunt, who brought her up, the obligations she was under to her, and the love she had for her little cousins, till the tears would stream down her cheeks; and how I had been her friend, and she loved me. Her papa would break her heart by making her go again. She clung round me so that I could not help shedding a tear at parting with her. She was a favorite of every one in the house. I regret that such fine spirits must be spent in the walls of a convent. She is a beautiful girl, too.[8]

Ursula was Mrs. Randolph's nurse. She was a big, fat woman. She took charge of all the children that were not in school. If there was any switching to be done, she always did it. She used to be down at my house a great deal with those children. They used to be there so much that we very often got tired of them; but we never said so. They were all very much attached to their nurse. They always called her "Mammy."[9]

John Hemings was a carpenter. He was a first-rate

workman—a very extra workman. He could make anything that was wanted in woodwork. He learned his trade of Dinsmore. He made most of the woodwork of Mr. Jefferson's fine carriage. Joe Fosset made the ironwork. He was a very fine workman; could do anything it was necessary to do with steel or iron. He learned his trade of Stewart. Mr. Jefferson kept Stewart several years longer than he would otherwise have done in order that his own servants might learn his trade thoroughly. Stewart was a very superior workman, but he would drink. And Burwell was a fine painter. He painted the carriage and always kept the house painted. He painted a good deal at the University.

Mr. Jefferson freed a number of his servants in his will.[10] I think he would have freed all of them if his affairs had not been so much involved that he could not do it. He freed one girl some years before he died, and there was a great deal of talk about it. She was nearly as white as anybody and very beautiful. People said he freed her because she was his own daughter. She was not his daughter; she was — —'s daughter. I know that. I have seen him come out of her mother's room many a morning when I went up to Monticello very early. When she was nearly grown, by Mr. Jefferson's direction I paid her stage fare to Philadelphia and gave her fifty dollars. I have never seen her since and don't know what became of her. From the time she was large enough, she always worked in the cotton factory. She never did any hard work."[11]

While Mr. Madison was President, one of our slaves ran away, and we never got him again. As soon as I learned that he was gone, I was satisfied that he had gone with Mr. Madison's cart to Washington and had passed himself off as Mr. Madison's servant. But Jeff Randolph did not believe it. He believed he had hid himself somewhere about the plantation, and he hunted everywhere for him. Finally he said he was sure he was hid in the loft of the stable where we kept our mules. I told him it was no use to look; but he would do it, and while crawling over the haymow, he tumbled through. I thought the mules would tread or kick him to death, but when he came out he said the mules were as badly scared as he was, when he fell among them, and did not move or hurt him at all. We afterwards learned that he went off with Mr. Madison's servant, as I had supposed. No servants ever had a kinder master than Mr. Jefferson's. He did not like slavery. I have heard him talk a great deal about it. He thought it a bad system. I have heard him prophesy that we should have just such trouble with it as we are having now.*

* Captain Bacon is a stanch Union man, utterly opposed to the whole secession movement. [Pierson's note.]

Mr. Jefferson at Washington — His Library

I VISITED Mr. Jefferson at Washington three times while he was President. My first visit was soon after his inauguration. I went to take his carriage horses. The second time I went he had got very much displeased with two of his servants, Davy and Fanny, and he wished me to take them to Alexandria and sell them. They were married and had got into a terrible quarrel. Davy was jealous of his wife, and, I reckon, with good reason. When I got there, they learned what I had come for, and they were in great trouble. They wept, and begged, and made good promises, and made such an ado, that they begged the old gentleman out of it. But it was a good lesson for them. I never heard any more complaint of them; and when I left Mr. Jefferson, I left them both at Monticello.

The last time I visited Mr. Jefferson in Washington, I stayed there sixteen days. This was when I went to help him settle up his business and move home his goods and servants.[1] He had eleven servants with him from Monticello. He had a French cook in Washington named Julien, and he took Eda and Fanny there to learn French cookery. He always preferred French cookery. Eda and Fanny were afterwards his cooks at Monticello.

Some days I was very busy attending to packing up his goods, getting in his bills, and settling up his business. Other days I had very little to do, and I would go up to the Capitol. I haven't been in Washington since the British played the wild there in the War of 1812. When I was there, the President's house was surrounded with a high rock wall, and there was an iron gate immediately in front of it, and from that gate to the Capitol the street was just as straight as a gun barrel. Nearly all the houses were on that street. I took a great deal of pleasure in going to the Capitol and hearing the debates.

Mr. Jefferson often told me that the office of Vice-President was far preferable to that of President. He was perfectly tired out with company. He had a very long dining room, and his table was chock-full every one of the sixteen days I was there. There were Congressmen, foreigners, and all sorts of people to dine with him. He dined at four o'clock, and they generally sat and talked until night. It used to worry me to sit so long, and I finally quit when I got through eating and went off and left them.[2]

The first thing in the morning there was to go to market. There was no market then in Washington. Mr. Jefferson's steward was a Frenchman named Lemaire. He was a very smart man, was well educated, and as much of a gentleman in his appearance as any man. His carriage driver was an Irishman named Daugherty. He would get out the wagon early in the morning, and Lemaire would go with him to Georgetown to market. I have all my life been in the habit of getting up about four o'clock in the morning, and I went with them very often. Lemaire told me that it often took fifty dollars to pay for what marketing they would use in a day.³ Mr. Jefferson's salary did not support him while he was President.

We got loaded up ready to start home, and I left Washington on the third of March. Mr. Jefferson stayed to attend the inauguration, but overtook us before we got home. I had three wagons from Monticello—two six-mule teams loaded with boxes, and the other four sorrel Chickasaw horses, and the wagon pretty much loaded with shrubbery from Maine's nursery. The servants rode on these wagons. I had the carriage horses and carriage, and rode behind them.

On our way home we had a tremendous snowstorm. It snowed very fast, and when we reached Culpeper Courthouse it was half-leg deep. A large crowd of people had collected there, expecting that the President would be along. When I rode up, they thought I was the President and shouted and hurrahed tremendously. When I got out of the carriage, they laughed very heartily at their mistake. There was a platform along the whole front of the tavern, and it was full of people. Some of them had been waiting a good while and drinking a good deal, and they made so much noise that they scared the horses, and Diomede backed, and tread upon my foot, and lamed me so that I could hardly get into the carriage the next morning. There was one very tall old fellow that was noisier that any of the rest, who said he was bound to see the President—"Old Tom," he called him. They asked me when he would be along, and I told them I thought he would certainly be along that night, and I looked for him every moment. The tavern was kept by an old man named Shackleford. I told him to have a large fire built in a private room, as Mr. Jefferson would be very cold when he got there, and he did so. I soon heard shouting, went out, and Mr. Jefferson was in sight. He was in a one-horse vehicle—a phaeton—with a driver and a servant on horseback. When he came up, there was great cheering again. I motioned to him to follow me; took him straight to his room and locked the door. The tall old fellow came and knocked very often, but I would not let him in. I told Mr. Jefferson not to mind him, he was drunk. Finally the door was opened, and they rushed in and filled the room. It was as full as I ever saw a barroom. He stood up and made a short address to them. Afterwards some of them told him how they had mistaken me for him. He went on next day and reached Monticello before we did, so that I did not see the large reception that the people of Albemarle gave him when he got home.*,4

---

* Mr. Jefferson was present at the inauguration of his successor, and soon afterwards [on March 11] set out for home. The inhabitants of the county of his birth and residence (Albemarle) had proposed to meet and escort him to Monticello, with imposing ceremonies. He quietly put aside the request, by declaring that he could not decide on the day of his return, and he added:

"But it is a sufficient happiness for me to know that my fellow-citizens of the country generally entertain for me the kind sentiments which have prompted this proposition, without giving to so many the trouble of leaving their homes to meet a single individual. I shall have opportunities of taking them individually by the hand at our Court House and other public places, and of exchanging assurances of mutual esteem. Certainly it is the greatest consolation to me to know, that in returning to the bosom of my native county, I shall be again in the midst of their kind affections; and I can say with truth

Mr. Jefferson had a very large library. When the British burnt Washington, the library that belonged to Congress was destroyed, and Mr. Jefferson sold them his. He directed me to have it packed in boxes and sent

---

that my return to them will make me happier than I have been since I left them."

The proposed ovation gave way to an address, and it was thus answered:

"TO THE INHABITANTS OF ALBEMARLE COUNTY, IN VIRGINIA

"April 3, 1809

"Returning to the scenes of my birth and early life, to the society of those with whom I was raised, and who have been ever dear to me, I receive, fellow-citizens and neighbors, with inexpressible pleasure, the cordial welcome you are so good as to give me. Long absent on duties which the history of a wonderful era made incumbent on those called to them, the pomp, the turmoil, the bustle and splendor of office, have drawn but deeper sighs for the tranquil and irresponsible occupations of private life, for the enjoyment of an affectionate intercourse with you, my neighbors and friends, and the endearments of family love, which nature has given us all, as the sweetener of every hour. For these I gladly lay down the distressing burden of power, and seek, with my fellow-citizens, repose and safety under the watchful cares, and labors, and perplexities, of younger and abler minds. The anxieties you express to administer to my happiness, do, of themselves, confer that happiness; and the measure will be complete, if my endeavors to fulfil my duties in the several public stations to which I have been called, have obtained for me the approbation of my country. The part which I have acted on the theatre of public life, has been before them, and to their sentence I submit it; but the testimony of my native county, of the individuals who have known me in private life, to my conduct in its various duties and relations, is the more grateful, as proceeding from eye-witnesses, and observers, from triers of the vicinage. Of you, then, my neighbors, I may ask, in the face of the world, "Whose ox have I taken, or whom have I defrauded? Whom have I oppressed, or of whose hand have I received a bribe to blind mine eyes herewith?" On your verdict I rest with conscious security. Your wishes for my happiness are received with just sensibility, and I offer sincere prayers for your own welfare and prosperity" (Randall's *Life of Jefferson*, III, 305–6). [Pierson's note.]

to Washington. John Hemings, one of his servants, made the boxes, and Burwell and I packed them up mostly. Dinsmore helped us some, and the girls, Ellen, Virginia, and Cornelia, would come in sometimes and sort them out and help us a good deal. There was an immense quantity of them. There were sixteen wagon-loads. I engaged the teams. Each wagon was to carry three thousand pounds for a load, and to have four dollars a day for delivering them in Washington. If they carried more than three thousand pounds, they were to have extra pay. There were all kinds of books—books in a great many languages that I knew nothing about. There were a great many religious books among them—more than I have ever seen anywhere else.[5] All the time Mr. Jefferson was President I had the keys to his library, and I could go in and look over the books, and take out any one that I wished, and read and return it. I have written a good many letters from that library to Mr. Jefferson in Washington. Mr. Jefferson had a sofa or lounge upon which he could sit or recline, and a small table on rollers, upon which he could write or lay his books. Sometimes he would draw this table up before the sofa and sit and read or write; and other times he would recline on his sofa, with his table rolled up the sofa, astride it. He had a large Bible, which nearly always lay at the head of his sofa. Many and many a time I have gone into his room and found him reading that Bible. You remember I told you about riding all night from Richmond, after selling that flour, and going into his room very early in the morning, and paying over to him the new United States Bank money. *That* was one of the times I found him with the big Bible open before him on his little table, and he busy reading it. And I have seen him reading it in that way many a time. Some people, you know, say he was an atheist. Now if he was an atheist, what did he want with all those religious books, and why did he spend so much of his time reading his Bible?

When Chancellor Wythe died, he willed to Mr. Jefferson his library. It was very large and nearly filled up the room of the one he sold to Congress.[6] Mr. Jefferson studied law with Chancellor Wythe. They thought a great deal of each other.

X

Mr. Jefferson's Hospitality

MR. JEFFERSON always had a great deal of company. He enjoyed seeing his friends very much. Mr. Madison was very often at Monticello. He generally stayed there when he attended court at Charlottesville. He was a fine man. He had a very solid look. I always thought he looked like a Methodist preacher; he wore his hair as they did then. Mr. Monroe, too, was at Monticello a great deal. I have seen him hundreds of times and done a great deal of business with him. I sold him the nails, from Mr. Jefferson's nailery, for his house.[1] I have had a great many letters from him. He was a miserable writer. Mr. Jefferson and Mr. Madison both wrote a plain beautiful hand, but you could write better with your toes than Mr. Monroe wrote. I have heard Gouverneur Morris say that once, after Mr. Monroe had transcribed a paper, he could not read it. (*Laughed heartily.*) Here are two of Mr. Monroe's letters:

Sir,—There has been a mistake in the kind of nails which I have written for. I cannot say whether you or I have made it. I wanted sixteenpenny nails, and eight-penny. Mr. Fogg will want some of the latter kind for his hog'ds, which I will thank you to add to those already written for.

I expect to pay you the cash at Court, or to make an arrangement to suit you.

Your very obedient servant,

JAS. MONROE

Mr. Bacon
January 8, 1810

Sir, — I have rec'd, by the boy, three pounds of nineteen and seven pence, the balance due me of the fifty dollars sent you this morning, after paying £11 0s. 5d. due Mr. Jefferson for nails. The statement is perfectly correct, and I am happy that it was in my power to accommodate you with the money.

I am respectfully yours,
JAS. MONROE

Feb. 7, 1810

Mr. Monroe was an indifferent manager — was nearly always in debt. He once applied to me to oversee for him and offered me more than Mr. Jefferson was paying me; but I said, "Sir, I would not leave Mr. Jefferson for any price." "Then," said he, "you must help me to get a man. You know what I want." I recommended a man to him, and he employed him.

Mr. Monroe was not the equal of Mr. Jefferson or Mr. Madison; and Chapman Johnson, Vaul W. Southall, William F. Gordon, and Phil Barbour were enough better lawyers than he. Everybody knew that. But he made the purchase of Louisiana, and that made him President. It was thought that he managed that matter remarkably well. I well remember the firing of guns and great rejoicings there were when the news of that purchase first came. It made Mr. Monroe so popular that he was elected President almost without opposition.

It used to be very interesting to the people to see the three ex-Presidents together. I have often seen them meet at Charlottesville on court day and stand and talk together a few minutes, and crowds of people would gather around them and listen to their conversation and follow them wherever they would go. I remember one court day I had been helping Scott, the Kentucky drover, sell his mules, as I knew all the people. He made fine sales that day, and when he had got through, he felt remarkably well and insisted on treating the company. When he came out of the barroom he saw a large crowd collected together and wanted to know what it meant. I told him Mr. Jefferson, Mr. Madison, and Mr. Monroe were there. "The three Virginia Presidents!" he shouted, and off he ran to see them. I have seen two other Presidents, Jackson and John Quincy Adams. Adams was a fine little fellow. He had a solid look.

After Mr. Jefferson returned from Washington, he was for years crowded with visitors, and they almost ate him out of house and home. They were there all times of the year; but about the middle of June the travel would commence from the lower part of the state to the Springs, and then there was a perfect throng of visitors. They traveled in their own carriages and came in gangs—the whole family, with carriage and riding horses and servants; sometimes three or four such gangs at a time. We had thirty-six stalls for horses, and only used about ten of them for the stock we kept there. Very often all of the rest were full, and I had to send horses off to another place. I have often sent a wagonload of hay up to the stable, and the next morning there would not be enough left to make a hen's nest. I have killed a fine beef, and it would all be eaten in a day or two. There was no tavern in all that country that had so much company. Mrs. Randolph, who always lived with Mr. Jefferson after his return from Washington and kept house for him, was very often greatly perplexed to entertain them. I have known her many and many a time to have every bed in the house full, and she would send to my wife and borrow all her beds—she had six spare beds—to accommodate her visitors. I finally told the servant who had charge of the stable to only give the visitors' horses half allowance. Somehow or other Mr. Jefferson heard of this; I never could tell how, unless it was through some of the visitors' servants. He countermanded my orders.[2]

One great reason why Mr. Jefferson built his house at Poplar Forest, in Bedford County, was that he might go there in the summer to get rid of entertaining so much company. He knew that it more than used up all his income from the plantation and everything else, but he was so kind and polite that he received all his visitors with a smile and made them welcome. They pretended to come out of respect and regard to him, but *I think* that the fact that they saved a tavern bill had a good deal to do with it with a good many of them. I can assure you I got tired of seeing them come and waiting on them. I knew just as much about Mr. Jefferson's business as he did himself, and I knew that he could not stand it long. You know that he failed. This was after I left him, but I knew that it was bound to come. He had to pay $20,000 for Governor Wilson C. Nicholas, whose daughter Jeff Randolph married. I knew all about that matter. I went to see Governor Nicholas a good many times on that business. Mr. Jefferson struggled on with that $20,000 several years, but that and his company finally broke him. After Governor Nicholas broke, he came to live with Jeff Randolph and died there. I helped lay out his corpse and had his grave dug.[3]

When the Governor died, he was very much in debt. People that he owed did not believe he was dead—they thought it was a trick to get rid of them. They came long distances and would come to see me about it, and I had hard work to make them believe that he was dead and buried. While he was governor, he once sent out an agent to meet the droves of hogs that were coming in to Richmond and buy them up; and the butchers were compelled to buy them all of him. They were so mad that he had taken this way to make money out of them that one night they covered the fence with hogs's entrails all around his house. After that they used to call him the "Hog Governor."

When I left Mr. Jefferson, his grandson, Jeff Randolph, took my place. He took charge of the business just as I had done for twenty years. I have loaned him money a great many times, and he has given me his note. Here is one of his notes, that is only part paid:

$900. On or before the first day of October, eighteen hundred and nineteen, I promise to pay Edmund Bacon, his heirs, executor, administrator, or assigns, the sum of nine hundred dollars, with legal interest from the twelfth day of October, 1818, to the true payment of which I bind myself, my heirs, executor, and administrator.

Witness my hand and seal, this eighth (8) day of November, 1818.

Th. J. Randolph [Seal.]

This note is endorsed on the back as follows:

Received from Thomas J. Randolph the sum of five hundred and fourteen dollars, in part of the within obligation.

E. Bacon

Sept. 20, 1819

I knew Jeff Randolph as well as one man can know another. Mr. Jefferson took great pains with his education, but he didn't take after his mother—he wasn't a Jefferson—he wasn't talented. He never wrote those letters about Mr. Jefferson without help. I know him too well to believe that. He never saw the day that he could write those letters. I should like to see him again. I know we should take a good deal of pleasure talking over old times.[4]

I was very sorry to leave Mr. Jefferson; but I was more willing to do it, because I did not wish to see the poor old gentleman suffer, what I knew he must suffer, from the debts that were pressing upon him. I know that he thought a great deal of me. I had proofs enough of that, besides the letter I showed you. I know that if one man ever tried to serve another faithfully, I did him—and he was satisfied. One day he was at the blacksmith shop, and — — found some fault with me and said my salary was too large. The blacksmith, who heard the conversation, told me of it, and said Mr. Jefferson replied, "Not one man in a thousand would do as well for me as Mr. Bacon has done."

When we parted, it was a trying time to me.[5] I don't know whether he shed any tears or not, but I know that I shed a good many. He was sitting in his room, on his sofa, where I had seen him so often, and keeping hold of my hand some time, he said, "Now let us hear from each other occasionally"; and as long as he lived I heard from him once or twice a year. The last letter I ever had from him was when I wrote him of the death of my wife, soon after I got to this country. He expressed a great deal of sympathy for me; said he did not wonder that I felt completely broken up and was disposed to move back; that he had passed through the same himself; and only time and silence would relieve me. That is the letter I told you I so much regretted I had lost.

I am now (1862) in my seventy-seventh year. I have seen a great many men in my day, but I have never seen the equal of Mr. Jefferson. He may have had the faults that he has been charged with, but if he had, I could never find it out. I don't believe that, from his arrival to maturity to the present time, the country has ever had another such a man.

Appendix

Mr. Jefferson's Will

I THOMAS JEFFERSON of Monticello, in Albemarle, being of sound mind and in my ordinary state of health, make my last will and testament, in manner and form as follows.

I give to my grandson Francis Eppes, son of my dear deceased daughter Mary Eppes, in fee simple, all that part of my lands at Poplar Forest lying west of the following lines, to wit, Beginning at Radford's upper corner near the double branches of Bear creek and the public road, & running thence in a straight line to the fork of my private road, near the barn, thence along that private road (as it was changed in 1817.) to it's crossing of the main branch of North Tomahawk creek, and from that crossing, in a direct line over the main ridge which divides the North and South Tomahawk, to the South Tomahawk, at the confluence of two branches where the old road to the Waterlick crossed it, and from that confluence up the Northernmost branch (which separates McDaniel's and Perry's fields) to it's source, & thence by the shortest line to my Western boundary. And having, in a former correspondence with my deceased son in law John W. Eppes contemplated laying off for him with remainder to my grandson Francis, a certain portion in the Southern part of my lands in Bedford and Campbell, which I afterwards found to be generally more indifferent than I had supposed, & therefore determined to change it's location for the better; now to remove all doubt, if any could arise on a purpose merely voluntary & unexecuted, I hereby declare that what I have herein given to my sd. grandson

Francis is instead of, and not additional to what I had formerly contemplated.

I subject all my other property to the payment of my debts in the first place.

Considering the insolvent state of the affairs of my friend & son in law Thomas Mann Randolph, and that what will remain of my property will be the only resource against the want in which his family would otherwise be left, it must be his wish, as it is my duty, to guard that resource against all liability for his debts, engagements or purposes whatsoever, and to preclude the rights, powers and authorities over it which might result to him by operation of law, and which might, independently of his will, bring it within the power of his creditors, I do hereby devise and bequeath all the residue of my property real and personal, in possession or in action, whether held in my own right, or in that of my dear deceased wife, according to the powers vested in me by deed of settlement for that purpose, to my grandson Thomas J. Randolph, & my friends Nicholas P. Trist and Alexander Garret & their heirs during the life of my sd. son in law Thomas M. Randolph, to be held & administered by them, in trust, for the sole and separate use and behoof of my dear daughter Martha Randolph and her heirs. And, aware of the nice and difficult distinctions of the law in these cases, I will further explain by saying, that I understand and intend the effect of these limitations to be, that the legal estate and actual occupation shall be vested in my said trustees, and held by them in base fee, determinable on the death of my sd. son in law, and the remainder during the same time be vested in my sd. daughter and her heirs, and of course disposable by her last will, and that at the death of my sd. son in law, the particular estate of the sd. trustees shall be determined, and the remainder, in legal estate, possession and use become vested in my said daughter and her heirs, in absolute property forever.

In consequence of the variety and indescribableness of the articles of property within the house at Monticello, and the difficulty of inventorying and appraising them separately and specifically, and it's inutility, I dispense with having them inventoried and appraised; and it is my will that my executors be not held to give any security for the administration of my estate. I appoint my grandson Thomas Jefferson Randolph my sole executor during his life, and after his death, I constitute executors my friends Nicholas P. Trist and Alexander Garret joining to them my daughter Martha Randolph after the death of my sd. son in law Thomas M. Randolph.

Lastly I revoke all former wills by me heretofore made; and in witness that this is my will, I have written the whole with my own hand on two pages and have subscribed my name to each of them this 16th day of March one thousand eight hundred and twenty six

TH. JEFFERSON

I Thomas Jefferson of Monticello in Albemarle make and add the following Codicil to my will, controuling the same so far as it's provisions go.

I recommend to my daughter, Martha Randolph, the maintenance and care of my well-beloved sister Anne Scott Marks, and trust confidently that from affection to her, as well as for my sake, she will never let her want a comfort.

I have made no specific provision for the comfortable maintenance of my son in law Thomas M. Randolph, because of the difficulty and uncertainty of devising terms which shall vest any beneficial interest in him which the law will not transfer to the benefit of his creditors, to the

destitution of my daughter and her family and disable-
ment of her to supply him: whereas property placed under
the exclusive control of my daughter and her independent
will, as if she were a femme sole, considering the relation
in which she stands both to him and his children, will be a
certain resource against want for all.

I give to my friend James Madison of Montpellier my
gold-mounted walking staff of animal horn, as a token of
the cordial and affectionate friendship which for nearly
now an half century, has united us in the same principles
and pursuits of what we have deemed for the greatest good
of our country.

I give to the University of Virginia my library, except
such particular books only, and of the same edition, as it
may already possess, when this legacy shall take effect. The
rest of my said library remaining after those given to the
University shall have been taken out, I give to my two
grandsons in law Nicholas P. Trist and Joseph Coolidge.

To my grandson Thomas Jefferson Randolph I give my
silver watch in preference of the golden one, because of it's
superior excellence. My papers of business going of course
to him, as my executor, all others of a literary or other
character I give to him as of his own property.

I give a gold watch to each of my grandchildren, who
shall not have already recieved one from me, to be
purchased and delivered by my executor, to my grandsons
at the age of 21. and granddaughters at that of sixteen.

I give to my good, affectionate, and faithful servant
Burwell his freedom, and the sum of three hundred
Dollars to buy necessaries to commence his trade of painter
and glazier, or to use otherwise as he pleases. I give also
to my good servants John Hemings and Joe Fosset, their
freedom at the end of one year after my death: and to each

of them respectively all the tools of their respective shops or callings: and it is my will that a comfortable log-house be built for each of the three servants so emancipated on some part of my lands convenient to them with respect to the residence of their wives, and to Charlottesville and the University, where they will be mostly employed, and reasonably convenient also to the interests of the proprietor of the lands; of which houses I give the use of one, with a curtilage of an acre to each, during his life or personal occupation thereof.

I give also to John Hemings the service of his two apprentices, Madison and Eston Hemings, until their respective ages of twenty one years, at which period respectively, I give them their freedom. And I humbly and earnestly request of the legislature of Virginia a confirmation of the bequest of freedom to these servants, with permission to remain in this state where their families and connections are, as an additional instance of the favor, of which I have recieved so many other manifestations, in the course of my life, and for which I now give them my last, solemn, and dutiful thanks.

In testimony that this is a Codicil to my will of yesterday's date, and that it is to modify so far the provisions of that will, I have written it all with my own hand, in two pages, to each of which I subscribe my name this 17th. day of March one thousand eight hundred and twenty six.

TH. JEFFERSON

Notes to the *Memoirs*

1 Isaac's mother was Ursula. His father was called "Great George" as well as "King George." At Monticello he was a blacksmith, nail maker, and first manager of the Monticello nailery. For other allusions to Ursula, see Edmund Bacon's comments in Hamilton W. Pierson, *Jefferson at Monticello: The Private Life of Thomas Jefferson* (New York, 1862). References to Bacon in subsequent notes are to this work, which forms the second part of the present volume.

2 Martha (Patsy) Jefferson was the eldest daughter of John Wayles, a native of Lancaster, England, who settled at The Forest, his home in Charles City County, Va. She married first Bathurst Skelton, who died in 1768, and after a widowhood of three years wed Thomas Jefferson (hereafter referred to as TJ) on Jan. 1, 1772. The Jeffersons had six children: three died in early infancy, a fourth, Lucy, at two years, but Martha (Patsy) and Mary (Maria, Polly) lived to adulthood. It is doubtful that Ursula was Martha's wet nurse at the same time she was nursing her own son. Martha was born in 1772 and Isaac not until 1775.

3 She married her third cousin, Thomas Mann Randolph, Jr., Feb. 23, 1790. Their home after 1800 was Edgehill, an Albemarle County farm. The family moved to Monticello in 1809, when Martha assumed the duties of housekeeper for her father.

4 There were two carpenters at Monticello named Neilson, Nielson, or Nelson. John worked there from 1805 until 1809.

5 William Orr was the Monticello blacksmith in 1782 and 1783.

6 Davy Watson was a house joiner by trade, though he worked at Monticello as a carriage maker. Probably he also performed other kinds of carpentry. His tenure began about April 1782 and continued until the fall of 1793.

7 The first Monticello house was begun about 1769 and finished in 1782. Isaac is chiefly concerned with this dwelling in his description of life at Monticello. Renovations were begun in 1793, and by 1809 this "first house" had become the present-day Monticello.

8 We know that Jefferson installed lightning rods on the first house, for on Aug. 21, 1780, he noted in an Account Book "Pd. Richardson mendg. lightening rod £12."
   TJ kept his accounts in a series of small notebooks, which cover the years 1767 to 1826. The originals are now in the possession of various libraries and historical societies. Photocopies of the series may be found in the Alderman Library of the University of Virginia.

9 There is no other evidence that TJ sent this or any other wheeled vehicle to London.

10 This remarkable family included a number of very able craftsmen and artisans. John Hemings is perhaps the best known, for he is believed to have made much of the furniture produced in the Monticello cabinet shop during TJ's lifetime. James was an excellent cook; he learned his trade when he was in France with TJ. Bacon also comments on John Hemings'

ability as a craftsman. A genealogical table of the Hemings family prepared by John Cook Wyllie, the best-versed scholar on slavery at Monticello, may be found following p. 24.

[11] Robert Hemings was manumitted Dec. 24, 1794. In Richmond he apparently lived and worked for Dr. George Frederick Strauss, marrying one of the doctor's slaves.

[12] See the genealogical table of the Hemings family.

[13] Actually Sally was fourteen when she and Mary (Polly), aged eight years, sailed from a Virginia harbor for France in May 1787, almost three years after TJ went.

[14] "The College" was the College of William and Mary. Lord Botetourt was colonial governor of Virginia from 1768 until 1770.

[15] The Rev. William Douglas, a Scottish clergyman, operated a school in Goochland County. TJ attended this school as a boy.

[16] On July 23, 1777, TJ noted: "Pd. Giovanni the taylor 36/" (Account Book).

[17] There is no known portrait of Mrs. Thomas Jefferson and most descriptions of her are too brief to be satisfactory. Isaac says the daughter Mary was pretty "like her mother."

[18] Isaac's mother, Ursula, may have derived her name from Ursula Byrd of Westover.

[19] There is no evidence in the several delineations of Eppes that he had a harelip.

[20] Isaac is the only contemporary who has described TJ as a fast driver.

[21] The state government moved to Richmond from Williamsburg in the spring of 1780.

[22] This "palace" should not be confused with the rather elegant structure in Williamsburg which had previously served as the governor's mansion. The Richmond palace was a ramshackle frame house which in 1780 needed repairs. Edward Dumbauld, *Thomas Jefferson, American Tourist* (Norman, Okla., 1946), believes it unlikely that TJ ever lived in this building.

[23] TJ's accounts list a number of transactions with one Wiley, a Richmond merchant. Presumably he is the "Billy Wiley" Isaac refers to.

[24] The invading British force under Benedict Arnold entered Richmond about 1:00 P.M. on Friday, Jan. 5, 1781. Early that morning TJ had taken his family to the safety of his property on Fine Creek about eight miles up the river from Richmond. Until the British departed on Jan. 6, TJ was at Westham, Manchester, and elsewhere occupied with public matters.

[25] Possibly James Marsden, a Richmond merchant.

[26] Lt. Col. James Graves Simcoe of the British army. At this time he commanded a detachment under Cornwallis.

[27] I have seen no evidence to substantiate Isaac's claim concerning the freeing of his father, George. However, among TJ's "taxable property in Albemarle" in 1782 were "129 slaves. 2. free" (Account Book, April 15, 1782). Since the freed ones are not identified, perhaps George was one of them.

[28] In 1871 it was located at the east end of Grace Street.

[29] Isaac to the contrary notwithstanding, the British went only to Westham (about ten miles) before returning to Richmond. On the morning of the sixth they burned certain houses and stores before departing about noon.

[30] Perhaps the oldest frame residence on the James River west of Richmond, Tuckahoe was begun by Thomas Mann Randolph, Sr., about 1715.

[31] Isaac was about six years old at this time.

[32] Isaac and the other Richmond household servants were apparently taken from Richmond to the Tidewater area and eventually to Yorktown, where they remained until after the British laid down their arms Oct. 19, 1781.

[33] TJ was thrown from his horse, injuring his right arm, sometime in the latter part of June. This injury gave rise to the tale conjured up by detractors that TJ was in such a hurry to flee Monticello and the British that he fell from his horse and broke his arm.

[34] Compare with Bacon's description of TJ and his remarks concerning TJ's dress.

[35] It is doubtful that Patrick Henry was a frequent visitor to Monticello, except possibly when the legislature met in Charlottesville.

[36] Dr. Thomas Walker, a prominent citizen of Albemarle County, Va., lived at Castle Hill, his estate, about six miles from TJ's birthplace, Shadwell. John, his oldest son, lived at Belvoir, in the vicinity of the present-day Grace Episcopal Church of Cismont, Albemarle County.

[37] Isaac, Bacon, and TJ's grandson, Thomas Jefferson Randolph, differ somewhat in their descriptions of TJ's daily routine. All agree that he arose early, generally before sunup. Randolph notes that after rising "at dawn, [TJ] wrote and read until breakfast." "After breakfast [he] read for half an hour in his public rooms or portico, in summer — visited his garden and workshops — returned to his writing and reading till one, when he rode on horseback to three or half past — dined, and gave the evening to his family and company—retired at nine, and to bed from ten to eleven" (Henry S. Randall, *The Life of Jefferson* [New York, 1858], III, App. XXXVI, 675; see also Bacon's comments).

[38] "Upstairs" was probably the library of the first Monticello house, which was located on the second floor over the parlor. This parlor was in the same area as the present one.

[39] Isaac's "copyin' machine" was a polygraph, of which TJ had three. One has survived and may be seen at Monticello.

[40] The implication here is that there was a mechanical dumb-waiter in TJ's bedroom or possibly in the library. There is no evidence to substantiate Isaac's statement. We know there were three mechanical dumb-waiters in Monticello: one in each end of the dining room mantel reaching down to the wine room and a third of shelves attached to the dining room door opposite the stairs leading up from the kitchen. There is, however, no crank in any of these dumb-waiters, all of which have been restored.

[41] The library of the first house had shelving for approximately 2,000 volumes. There were about 6,000 books in the "Great Library," which was sold to the federal government in 1815. Isaac could have seen TJ in both libraries (Randolph G. Adams, *Three Americanists* [Philadelphia, 1939]).

[42] A house was built at Colle in Albemarle County about 1770 by Philip Mazzei, who, while living there, attempted unsuccessfully to adapt European grapes to its red-clay slopes. Mazzei stayed at Monticello until his house was finished.

[43] Baron de Riedesel, who was captured by the Americans at Saratoga, lived at Colle with his family from 1779 to 1780.

[44] The vegetable garden was regraded in 1810 into an area about 1,000 by 80 feet. It comprised three terraces (actually long steps) which led up from the barn on the eastern end.

[45] In 1817 TJ paid a Mr. Logan for working on the following clocks at Monticello: "To wit. Kitchen clock 4.*d*. black marble do. 4.*d*. white marble do. 5.*d*. great do. 9–32" (Account Book, Feb. 15).

[46] The large number of guests and family reported as being at Monticello causes one to wonder whether TJ ever dined alone.

[47] Much has been written about TJ and wine, but little concerning his own consumption of it. Isaac's reference is one of few. TJ himself wrote: "I double, however, the Doctor's [Benjamin Rush's?] glass and a half of wine, and even treble it with a friend; but halve its effects by drinking weak wines only" (letter to Dr. Vine Utley, March 21, 1819, Andrew A. Lipscomb and Albert E. Bergh, eds., *The Writings of Thomas Jefferson* [Washington, 1903], XV, 187).

[48] TJ was a fine amateur violinist according to many contemporary accounts. He has admitted that he played and practiced several hours each day until he broke his right wrist in Paris in 1786.

[49] There was always a keyboard instrument, chiefly for Martha's use, at Monticello. She took lessons on the guitar and harpsichord when she was in Paris. Her harpsichord teacher was Claude Louis Balbastre, the celebrated French musician and teacher.

[50] There is no record in TJ's accounts of his having paid anyone named Fauble to tune any of the Monticello musical instruments.

[51] Bacon also remembered TJ's singing.

[52] Isaac's memory appears to have failed him somewhat as he recounted this incident in his life. He probably started an apprenticeship during the early 1790's in Philadelphia with James Bringhurst, TJ's ironmonger acquaintance, and he returned to Monticello in 1794, for his name appears on the slave roll that year. He seems to have confused the jobs of Secretary of State and the Presidency because he mistakes TJ's reason for going to Philadelphia in 1790. Isaac further errs in recalling TJ's having lived in Washington's one-time residence. Washington lived in the Robert Morris house, whereas TJ first rented Thomas Leiper's house and, later, one at Gray's Ferry on the Schuylkill River outside the city. The large brick house with many windows that Isaac recalls may have been the three-story brick building at 307 Market Street, then the offices of the Secretary of State.

[53] Isaac seems to be confused here. Mary (Polly) remained at Monticello with Martha and Thomas Mann Randolph, Jr., though she may have visited her aunt, Martha Jefferson Carr (Mrs. Dabney) at the Carr home, Spring Forest in Goochland County. Apparently both of the sisters spent some time at Eppington, the Chesterfield County, Va., home of another aunt, Elizabeth Eppes.

[54] James Bringhurst may have come to Monticello to assist in the establishment of a metalworking shop; however, his name does not appear in related Jefferson manuscripts as having been there.

[55] The Colonel died in 1787; hence Isaac's recollections of his visits were to the first Monticello house.

[56] Thomas Mann Randolph, Sr., married Anne (Nancy) Cary in 1761. She was the eldest of Colonel Archibald Cary's children.

[57] Ampthill was in Chesterfield County, just south of Richmond. Thomas Mann Randolph, Jr., took title to the Edgehill property from his father in 1793. Thomas Jefferson Randolph was his eldest son.

[58] Isaac's recollections here are amazingly accurate. In 1794 TJ established a nailery at Monticello for the commercial manufacture of nails. It was closed in 1823 after a fairly successful history. Isaac appears in the Nailery Account Book as a nail maker (*Thomas Jefferson's Farm Book*, ed. Edwin M. Betts [Philadelphia, 1953], 426–53 [hereafter cited as *Farm Book*], and James A. Bear, Jr., "Mr. Jefferson's Nails," *Magazine of Albemarle County History*, XVI [1957–58], 47–52).

[59] Milton is located at the head of navigation on the Rivanna River, a few miles south of Monticello. Once a thriving commercial center, it is today little more than a geographical expression.

[60] Actually, Thomas Mann Randolph, Jr., had twelve children, one of whom, Ellen Wayles Randolph, died within a year of her birth. The children are listed in Jefferson's prayer book in this order: Anne Cary, Thomas Jefferson, Ellen Wayles (I), Ellen Wayles (II), Cornelia, Virginia, Mary Jefferson, James, Benjamin, Lewis, Septimia, and George Wythe. Anne Cary, the eldest, was born in 1791; George Wythe, the youngest, twenty-seven years later.

[61] If William Branch Giles courted Mary (Polly), he did so before Oct. 13, 1797, when she married her cousin, John Wayles Eppes. Giles married Martha Tabb the same year. A difference in age may have affected his suit, for in 1796 he was thirty-four and Mary eighteen.

[62] TJ inherited both Elk Hill and Elk Island through his wife. Elk Island contained 330 acres and was situated in the James River opposite Elk Hill, a farm of 266 acres in Goochland County, Va. TJ's Account Books, which chronicle his whereabouts, do not support Isaac's report of the visits to Elk Hill, but there are *Farm Book* entries which might imply occasional visits there in the 1770's.

[63] The Account Book entries substantiate Isaac's comment that TJ had a number of firearms. Among these was a "double barreled gun," purchased for 60 francs in Paris (Account Book, July 12, 1787). TJ viewed hunting, as he did many other pursuits, through his utilitarian eye: "As to the species of exercise, I advise the gun. While this gives a moderate exercise to the body, it gives boldness, enterprize, and independance to the mind" (letter to Peter Carr, Aug. 19, 1785, Julian P. Boyd, ed., *The Papers of Thomas Jefferson* (Princeton, N.J., 1950–), VIII, 407 (hereafter cited as Boyd, ed., *Papers*).

[64] Isaac refers to the first, or 1782, house.

[65] Isaac is speaking of the Gilbert Stuart painting known as the "Edgehill Portrait" which Gimbrede engraved for use in William Linn, *The Life of Thomas Jefferson* (Ithaca, N.Y., 1834).

[66] TJ called the school building the South Out Chamber or the South Pavilion. It is the terminal building of the south terrace walk, which connects it with the main house. The South Octagon was the southernmost room in the first Monticello house.

[67] Probably Anne Wayles (Mrs. Henry) Skipwith of Hors du Monde in Cumberland County, Va., and her sister Elizabeth Wayles (Mrs. Francis) Eppes of Eppington.

[68] John Bolling married TJ's sister, Mary. They lived at Chestnut Grove in Chesterfield County.

[69] Willis' Mountain is in Buckingham County, Va., about forty miles from Monticello. Isaac's description of the mountain's appearance involves an optical phenomenon called "looming."

[70] The "Catalogue of Paintings &c. at Monticello," compiled by TJ about 1809 and now at the University of Virginia, records 137 individual works of art — paintings, engravings, silhouettes, statuary, etc. — in the house at this time. TJ had at least six delineations of Washington and three of Lafayette.

[71] Isaac was a small boy when he first saw Lafayette because he was only about six when the Battle of Yorktown took place. Lafayette visited Monticello for the last time in 1825.

[72] A large marble pedestal stood in the Entrance Hall at Monticello and held the Ceracchi bust of TJ. After TJ's death both the bust and the

pedestal were sold to the federal government and placed in the Library of Congress. The bust and the pedestal were destroyed in 1851 in the Library of Congress fire.

73 TJ purchased reading glasses while in France in 1787. On Dec. 6, 1793, he bought a pair of spectacles from William Richardson in Philadelphia. Early in 1794 he characterized his health as being in "a bad state" and by Sept. 7 he informed Edmund Randolph that he was "under a paroxysm of rheumatism which has now kept me for ten days in constant torment, and presents no hope of abatement" (Lipscomb and Bergh, eds., *op. cit.*, IX, 290).

74 Bacon also comments on John Hemings as a carpenter.

75 Lucy, TJ's youngest daughter, died at Eppington in 1784 of the whooping cough.

76 TJ's interest in watching horse races is recorded in the following Account Book entries: Aug. 11, 1769; Nov. 30 and Dec. 1, 1802; Nov. 9, 10, 11, 1803; and Oct. 29, 30, 31, 1805. There is no evidence that he gambled on the races or that he raced his own horses.

77 According to TJ's accounts, Brimmer was purchased from Carter Braxton of King William Couny, Va., on Oct. 4, 1790, and sold to Samuel Clarkson of Staunton for $120 on Feb. 1, 1793. Bacon mistakenly identifies Bremo as Brimmer. Perhaps Isaac was thinking of Matchless, who, while being ridden by the servant Joseph in Philadelphia, ran into a wagon shaft and killed himself (TJ to Thomas Mann Randolph, Jr., Feb. 18, 1793, Jefferson Papers, Library of Congress).

78 An Account Book entry for March 10, 1790, is of interest: "Recd here Mr. W. Fitzhugh's horse Tarquin. 9. or 10 years old. Got by Eclipse out of Peyton Randolph's roan mare who was of the blood of monkey, Othello & Dabster. I am to pay £75. excels in 2. mile heats. 140 lb."

79 Davy Watson and William (Billy) Orr were deserters from the British army. Isaac was correct about their drinking prowess.

80 Rabbits are strangely absent from the farm and garden books as being domesticated animals at Monticello.

81 As a youth TJ certainly danced, despite what Isaac, and also Bacon, report of his later years. Even as an older man he subscribed to balls and dancing assemblies in Georgetown, Washington, and Philadelphia. He also saw that his children and grandchildren learned to dance. There is no evidence that he played cards.

82 TJ appears to have preferred sheep dogs or those who could render useful farm service. For his varying reactions to dogs see his letters to Bacon, Dec. 26, 1808 (Jefferson Papers, Huntington Library, San Marino, Calif.) and to Peter Minor, Sept. 24, 1811 (Jefferson Papers, Massachusetts Historical Society). He told Minor he would require every dog to "wear a collar with the name of the person inscribed who shall be security for his honest demeanor."

83 Additional information about John Brock appears in the Account Book entries for Jan. 29 and March 11, 1778, and April 27 and May 14, 1779. His position at Monticello is not clear.

84 The Account Book for 1771 gives the plans for the park. When the Marquis de Chastellux visited Monticello in 1782, he noted that "Mr. Jefferson [had] amused himself by raising a score of these animals [deer] in a park" (*Travels in North America,* ed. Howard C. Rice, Jr. [Chapel Hill, N.C., 1963], II, 394).

85 Isaac may have mistaken wild dogs for wolves.

86 Isaac has confused the children of Peter and Jane Jefferson with those

of John Wayles. The children of Jane and Peter Jefferson were Jane (1740–65); Mary (1741–1817), married John Bolling; Thomas (1743–1826), married Martha Wayles Skelton; Elizabeth (1744–74); Martha (1746–1811), married Dabney Carr; Peter Field (1748–48); an unnamed son (1750–50); Lucy (1752–84), married Charles L. Lewis; Anna Scott (1755–1828), married Hastings Marks; and Randolph (1755–1815), married Anne Jefferson Lewis (died ca. 1808) and Mitchie B. Pryor.

According to Jefferson's family Bible, John Wayles, TJ's father-in-law, had four daughters by two wives: the first wife was Martha Eppes, the mother of Martha Wayles Jefferson; the second was a Miss Cocke, the mother of Elizabeth Wayles (Mrs. Francis) Eppes, Tabitha Wayles (Mrs. Robert) Skipwith, and Anne Wayles (Mrs. Henry) Skipwith. There was no issue by his third wife, the widow of Reuben Skelton. The Bible indicates that Martha Wayles Jefferson had no full brothers or sisters who survived infancy: a brother and sister born Dec. 23, 1746, died the same day.

[87] Bernard Mayo, *Thomas Jefferson and His Unknown Brother* (Charlottesville, Va., 1942), provides the fullest account of Randolph Jefferson's life.

[88] John Wayles Eppes married first Mary (Polly) Jefferson; they lived variously at Eppington, Bermuda Hundred, and Mount Blanco, Chesterfield County. His second marriage was to another cousin, Mary Elizabeth Cleland Randolph. They lived at Millbrook, Buckingham County.

[89] This would have been in 1822. The presence of several Isaacs at Monticello simultaneously (some hired, some owned; see *Farm Book*, pp. 50 and 52) makes it impossible to verify Isaac's statement. Isaac was deeded with his wife Iris and two children to TJ's daughter Mary in 1797, but in the following year he apparently joined the family of her sister, Martha Randolph.

[90] Campbell described Pocahontas as "a village on the Appomattox River, opposite Petersburg."

[91] The *Farm Book* provides additional information about how TJ fed and clothed his slaves.

[92] Bacon's statements about TJ's kindness to his staff support Isaac's judgment.

Notes to *The Private Life*

I

[1] Clopton was a student at the University of North Carolina in 1809 and at the same time held a tutorship. From 1812 until 1818 he was the director of a boys' preparatory school connected with the University of

North Carolina. He left Chapel Hill in 1819 (Jeremiah B. Jeter, *A Memoir of Abner W. Clopton, A.M., Pastor of Baptist Churches in Charlotte County, Virginia* [Richmond, 1837], 35–36, 69).

² The college referred to was Cumberland College, Princeton, Ky. Pierson was its president from 1858 to 1861 (M. H. Thomas, archivist at Princeton University, to J. A. Bear, July 26, 1966).

³ Bacon has telescoped the history of the Central College and the University of Virginia. He lists members of the Board of Visitors of the University and not of the Board of Commissioners, whose members selected the site of the University. The law enacted Feb. 21, 1818, charged the Commissioners to select a site "convenient and proper." There was no proviso referring to the Charlottesville courthouse. The Board with Jefferson in the chair selected the site of the Central College which had previously been established in Albemarle County (Philip A. Bruce, *History of the University of Virginia, 1819–1919* [New York, 1920–1922], I, 164–72, 209, 236, and Roy J. Honeywell, *The Educational Work of Thomas Jefferson* [Cambridge, Mass., 1931], App. J, "Report of the Commissioners Appointed to Fix the Site of the University of Virginia, etc.," 248–60).

⁴ Bruce does not support Bacon's statements concerning Nicholas Lewis' and John Craven's offers of lands. He traces the title of the tract which John Perry disposed of to the Visitors of the Central College. This, of course, was the site chosen by the Board of Commissioners meeting at a tavern at Rockfish Gap in the Blue Ridge Mountains on Aug. 1, 1818 (Bruce, *op cit.,* I, 167–72, and Honeywell, *op. cit.,* 248).

⁵ According to Edwin M. Betts, editor of the *Farm Book,* TJ's buying and selling of land after 1810 was limited, possibly because of his poor financial condition (324–25).

⁶ Bruce and Bacon are in general agreement concerning the laying off of the site. Bruce, *op. cit.,* I, 188, states that TJ staked out the plot in an open, worn-out field. The laying off was completed under his eye and "certainly partly, if not entirely, with his actual assistance." Ten men began the work of readying the area. James Dinsmore was an able carpenter who had done much of the work in remodeling Monticello. Later he was employed at the University.

⁷ TJ's role in these ceremonies is not commented upon by Bruce. TJ's hair during these years was not white but a soft, sandy reddish color.

⁸ It would be more correct to say that TJ's visits to the University were regular, rather than daily, over a long period of time.

II

¹ According to TJ, his estate was left in the hands of Col. Nicholas Lewis, of Albemarle County, and Francis Eppes, of Chesterfield County, Va. (letter to Alexander McCaul, April 19, 1786, Boyd, ed., *Papers*, IX, 389; see also XI, 10, 256).

² TJ's Account Book gives Sept. 29, 1806, as the time when Bacon began as manager-overseer; "I am indebted to Edmund Bacon for services to ys.

day 20.D. He agrees to serve me as manager one year from this day for 100.D. 600. lb. pork and half a beef." On Oct. 15, 1822, sixteen years later, TJ made this notation in one of his ever-present Account Books: "Had a final settlement with Edmund Bacon and paid him 41.90 the balance due him in full." If Bacon was born on March 28, 1785, then he would have been nearly sixteen years old at TJ's first inauguration and nearly twenty on March 4, 1805.

[3] TJ was at Poplar Forest from July 5 to 16, 1818. Recalling his reason for taking the waters at the Warm Springs to John Adams, Dec. 18, 1825, he wrote: "Being at that period [1818] in the neighborhood of our Warm springs, and well in health, I wished to be better, and tried them" (Lester J. Cappon, ed., *The Adams-Jefferson Letters* [Chapel Hill, N.C., 1959], II, 612). While at the springs he contracted an "imposthume and eruptions [on the buttocks] which with the torment of the journey back reduced me to the last stages of weakness and exhaustion" (letter to Francis Eppes, Sept. 11, 1818, Jefferson Papers, Huntington Library).

[4] Edward Coles was a brother of Isaac Coles, once TJ's secretary. James Monroe named him governor of the Illinois Territory (Edgar Woods, *Albemarle County in Virginia* [Bridgewater, Va., n.d.], 173).

[5] Bacon's horse was probably sired by TJ's Diomede. See *Farm Book*, 104, 108.

[6] William Clark was then governor of the Missouri Territory, with headquarters in St. Louis.

III

[1] Inasmuch as this chapter and those following are given almost entirely in Bacon's words (except for material quoted from TJ and others), the quotation marks around the text in the 1862 edition have been dropped. The few words interposed by Pierson are in italics and his notes are labeled.

[2] The house shown opposite p. 51 is a drawing of the finished version of Monticello. It is adapted from the George Cooke delineation made in the early 1830's and until the advent of photography was the most commonly reproduced (James A. Bear, Jr., *Old Pictures of Monticello* [Charlottesville, Va., 1957], 18).

[3] Isaac also describes the garden.

[4] Thomas Maine was an Alexandria nurseryman who introduced TJ to the Washington thorn. Four thousand of these were set out in 1805 in the south thorn hedge which circumscribed the orchard and part of the vegetable garden.

[5] William Stewart was TJ's able Monticello blacksmith from 1801 to 1807. His dismissal was due to intemperate use of alcohol.

[6] Probably Joe Fossett, an ironworker at Monticello who was manumitted under the terms of TJ's will.

[7] John H. Craven. The Account Book for Dec. 18, 1807, provides additional information about this transaction.

[8] John Kelly was the owner of land lying west of Charlottesville which was TJ's first choice as the location of the Central College. He refused to sell, apparently because of some resentment toward Jefferson. Bruce mentions this in his *History*, I, 167–68.

[9] This memorandum is quoted in Edwin M. Betts, ed., *Thomas Jefferson's Garden Book* (Philadelphia, 1944), 355–56 (hereafter cited as *Garden Book*).

[10] Jefferson had several slaves named Davy. This was probably Davy, Sr., a slave TJ inherited from his father-in-law in 1774.

[11] The 1809 survey for the Monticello roads and their relation to the house, the orchard, and vegetable garden terrace are pictured in Frederick D. Nichols, *Thomas Jefferson's Architectural Drawings* (Boston, 1960), No. 17.

[12] TJ's land roll reproduced in the *Farm Book* lists 10,647 acres in 1794 and 10,004⅙ in 1810. The Monticello tract at these times contained 1052¾ acres (*ibid.*, 32, 127, 324–25).

[13] Part of this information appears in the *Farm Book*, 426–28.

IV

[1] TJ conducted at least two experiments in sheep raising. The earliest, with the Merino breed, began about 1792. The second, with the Barbary broadtailed sheep of the Tripoline breed, was conducted about 1806 (*ibid.*, 111–42).

[2] Large amounts of pork and lard were consumed on TJ's farms, and the hog was an important farm animal. TJ mentions only the "pure breed of Guinea hogs" and a "boar pig of the Chinese or Parkinson breed" (*ibid.*, 144 and *passim*).

[3] Gen. Henry Dearborn was Secretary of War in the Jefferson cabinet.

[4] Very little is known about TJ and cattle raising. The *Farm Book* discusses the matter briefly on p. 111.

[5] This may refer to a carriage made at Monticello in 1814, the one for which the "15. yds. of scarlet rattinett" was purchased from William Richardson in Philadelphia (TJ to William Richardson, April 6, 1814, Jefferson Papers, Massachusetts Historical Society).

[6] The best treatment of TJ and his horses is in the *Farm Book*, 87–110. The Account Book, Dec. 6, 1808, states that Diomede was purchased by John Wayles Eppes from Richard Thweatt for $250. Isaac also mentions this. TJ paid David Isaacs $125 for Tecumseh (Account Book, June 14, 1815). Wellington, according to Jefferson's accounts, was "bought of Elias Wells [of Albemarle County] for 120.D." (*ibid.*, May 14, 1815). Eagle's name appears in the same source under Nov. 6, 1820.

[7] Isaac describes TJ's driving habits, horses, and modes of travel.

V

[1] TJ owned several mills on the Rivanna River below Monticello. One, a toll or grist mill built about 1757, he inherited from his father, Peter Jefferson. This was lost in the high waters of 1771 and was rebuilt about 1803. It was chiefly used for TJ's own needs. Plans for a merchant or manufacturing mill were made in 1793; however, it did not go into operation until 1807. Its first tenants were the Shoemakers, Jonathan and Isaac, father and son. This mill, which promised hope for TJ's sagging finances and assistance to the community, never realized its potential because of poor management, trouble with the lessees, and the ever-present maintenance costs for the mill house, dam, and canal. The mill, estimated by Betts to have cost $10,000, was almost a total loss. It was never successfully operated. The *Farm Book*, 341–411, covers in detail all of TJ's Rivanna River operations. The mills in this note have no relation to the so-called Peter Jefferson mill on the Hardware River near Scottsville in Albemarle County.

[2] Jefferson's Nailery Account Book, 1796–1800, is a combination of accounts, sales, and production figures. The original is in the William A. Clark Memorial Library, University of California at Los Angeles. Isaac also mentions the nailery.

[3] During the early days at Monticello, the common loom, the hand card, and the spinning wheel, plus slave labor, were the instruments for spinning and weaving cloth. The first spinning jenny was bought in 1812 from William McClure, and by 1814 four jennies were running. Three of these had twenty-four spindles and the other forty. For making coarse cloth there were two everyday looms with flying shuttles. The *Farm Book*, 464–95, describes this very necessary operation at Monticello and Poplar Forest.

[4] TJ's earliest smith's shop was on "the Shadwell Branch" below Monticello and was built about 1774. Francis Bishop was the first smith and Barnaby, a slave, his helper. Work appears to have been done here for all TJ's farms until 1790, when a shop was established on the Mulberry Row at Monticello. In 1793 it was combined with the nailery. The 1809 survey shows a smith's shop on the Second Round approximately 150 yards in front of the East Front of the house. William Stewart did much of his fine work in this shop. Presumably this building was removed soon after the house was completed in 1809.

[5] This was James Dinsmore, mentioned earlier. Burwell was a slave.

VI

[1] Bacon's description does not vary appreciably from those of others who knew TJ. Daniel Webster's description in 1824 is in Randall, *op. cit.*, III, 505–6, and that of the Marquis de Chastellux made in 1782 is found in his

Travels in North America, II, 391. The Duke de la Rochefoucauld-Liancourt observed in 1796: "In private life, Mr. Jefferson displays a mild, easy and obliging temper, though he is somewhat cold and reserved" (Randall, *op. cit.*, II, 302 ff) . Isaac also described TJ.

2 TJ owned a dynamometer, which may be the machine mentioned by Bacon. His superiority in muscle power over his son-in-law is not generally reported by his biographers. For a reference to the dynamometer see Thomas Mann Randolph, Jr., to TJ, Oct. 14, 1818 (University of Virginia) .

3 TJ undoubtedly had a strong constitution. Even so, he suffered from "periodical headaches," a visceral complaint, and sometimes severe rheumatic attacks before he died of the infirmities of old age at ten minutes before one o'clock on July 4, 1826. His letter to Dr. Vine Utley, March 21, 1819 (Lipscomb and Bergh, eds., *op. cit.*, XV, 186–88) gives an excellent summary of his health.

4 Bacon refers to the great flood of 1807, which swept away about a half of TJ's milldam. (See pp. 71–72.) The dam was repaired, and the manufacturing mill returned to production about 1809 (TJ to James Madison, Aug. 16, 1807, Jefferson Papers, Library of Congress, and to Martha Jefferson Randolph, Jan. 30, 1808, University of Virginia) .

5 All accounts of TJ's daily routine list him as an early riser. Isaac reports TJ never came out of his room until about 8:00 A.M.

6 As a youth TJ gambled at lotto, backgammon, cross and pyle, pitchers, and shooting (Account Books, March 18, 1769; Nov. 21, 1770; and Oct. 23, 1785) . He also danced as a youth, and as a father and grandfather he saw to it that the children in his family learned to dance. On this social grace he wrote Nathaniel Burwell: "[Dancing] is a necessary accomplishment, therefore, although of short use; for the French rule is wise, that no lady dances after marriage" (March 14, 1818, Lipscomb and Bergh, eds., *op. cit.*, XV, 167) . Isaac says TJ never danced or played cards.

7 TJ informed Dr. Vine Utley that he had "lived temperately, eating little animal food, and that not as an aliment, so much as a condiment for vegetables, which constitute my principal diet" (March 21, 1819, Lipscomb and Bergh, eds., *op. cit.*, XV, 187) .

8 Jefferson invented a moldboard for a plow. For this he was elected a foreign associate of the Society of Agriculture of France (*Farm Book*, 47–48) .

9 A granddaughter reported that he dressed plainly and simply, wearing what he wanted to. Often he wore long waistcoats when short ones were in vogue or stocks when cravats were stylish. He did not wear pantaloons until late in life (Sarah Nicholas Randolph, *The Domestic Life of Thomas Jefferson* [Charlottesville, Va., 1947], 337) . Thomas Jefferson Randolph, a grandson, wrote: "In early life, his dress, equipage and appointments were fastidiously appropriate to his rank. As he grew old, although preserving his extreme neatness, his dress was plainer, and he was more indifferent to the appearance of his equipage" (Randall, *op. cit.*, III, 674) .

10 TJ's benevolences to the poor and less fortunate may be noted on almost every page in his Account Books.

11 The name of this mule does not appear either in the *Farm Book* or in Account Books. The latter, however, do include such unmulelike names as "Captain Molly," "Doll Tweezer," "Dr. Slop," and "Ringdum Funnidos."

12 William Cabell Rives married Judith Walker of Albemarle County, but Hugh Nelson married Miss Eliza Kinloch of South Carolina.

13 The Account Book for Jan. 19, 1813, notes: "Recd. from Wm. Douglas

for firewood to Oct. 1. 12. 11.D." James Marr's name does not appear in the index of the Account Books.

14 An examination of available examples of Bacon's and TJ's signatures fails to show any similarity.

15 On Jan. 13, 1813, TJ wrote in his Account Book: "Richd. Durrett enters my service as carpenter."

VII

1 TJ had six children, four of whom died before they reached their third year. Mary died in 1804 and Martha in 1836. Only one of Mary's children lived past infancy, Francis Wayles Eppes.

2 Francis L. Berkeley, Jr., in his Introduction to the *Farm Book*, xiv, comments on TJ's habit of "habitually singing as he went, not the melodies chanted by his servants at work, but the more sophisticated music of Italy and France." Unfortunately neither Isaac nor Bacon identified any of TJ's songs.

3 Bacon's free access to TJ's living quarters is not supported by the various visitors' accounts or by Thomas Jefferson Randolph. He answered this claim of Bacon's (along with many others) in his broadside, "The Last Days of Jefferson" (about 1824, copy at University of Virginia) with these words: "The intimacy with Mr. Jefferson did not exist. Such intimacies rarely existed between overseers of even the highest class and their employers. Mr. Jefferson's room was his *sanctum sanctorum;* was always occupied and he never liked to be interrupted." Randolph states that his mother never sat in TJ's room.

4 For other descriptions of Martha Jefferson Randolph see Malone, *Jefferson and the Rights of Man,* 131; Edwin M. Betts and James A. Bear, Jr., eds., *The Family Letters of Thomas Jefferson* (Columbia, Mo., 1966), 4–5, 8; and Sarah Nicholas Randolph, "Mrs. Thomas Mann Randolph," in Mrs. O. J. Wister and Miss Agnes Irvin, eds., *Worthy Women of Our First Century* (Philadelphia, 1877), 16, 17, 23.

5 Thomas Jefferson Randolph had twelve children. See p. 127 n.60.

6 For additional information about TJ and his grandchildren see Barbara Mayo, "Twilight at Monticello," *Virginia Quarterly Review* (October 1941), VII, 502–16; S. N. Randolph, *Domestic Life;* and Betts and Bear, eds., *op. cit.*

7 Thomas Jefferson Randolph in his "The Last Days of Jefferson" disavows the William C. Rives episode at Monticello and particularly his "taking shelter in his [Bacon's] house from the libertine contamination of Mr. Jefferson's grandsons."

8 William H. Gaines, Jr., *Thomas Mann Randolph: Jefferson's Son-in-Law* (Baton Rouge, La., 1966), is the best study of "Mr. Randolph."

9 Thomas Jefferson Randolph denied such attacks.

10 Charles L. Bankhead was an intemperate drinker. Martha Randolph wrote that "the Capt. [Miller] will live with them at which I am delighted for they will always require a protector. Mr. Bankhead has begun to drink

again" (letter to TJ, Aug. 7, 1819, Betts and Bear, eds., *op. cit.*, 430).
Bankhead and Thomas Jefferson Randolph once engaged in a savage fight
on the courthouse square in Charlottesville in which Randolph was
severely wounded. Bankhead was arrested and posted bond but he was
never brought to trial (Joseph C. Vance, "Thomas Jefferson Randolph,"
61–75, unpublished dissertation, University of Virginia).

VIII

[1] Isaac bears this out as do many of the visitors' accounts in the
Descriptions of Monticello File at Monticello.

[2] TJ's treatment of his slaves has received scant scholarly study. A cursory
review of the Account Books and the *Farm Book* indicates that he bought,
sold, and hired them, and also had them flogged.

[3] Jame or Jamey Hubbard was not such a good servant that he refrained
from running away. If he was not whipped after the theft of the nails, he
was in April 1812 after he had run away to Pendleton County, Va. The
Grady mentioned in the text was probably Reuben Grady, a local resident
who occasionally sold TJ coal and wood.

[4] Before Bacon's arrival at Monticello, Jupiter was TJ's body servant. He
died in 1800 in Fredericksburg. Burwell outlived his master.

[5] According to the *Farm Book*, 135, there were twenty-five household
servants of all kinds at Monticello in 1810.

[6] Martha Wayles Jefferson died at Monticello on Sept. 6, 1782, at 11:45
A.M. at thirty-three years of age. She was survived by only three children:
Martha, Mary, and Lucy.

[7] Wine and cider were the only two alcoholic drinks TJ consumed.

[8] Printed in Charles F. Adams, ed., *Letters of Mrs. Adams, the Wife of
John Adams* (Boston, 1840), II, 179–80. A letter Abigail Adams wrote to
Jefferson about Mary and Polly is in Cappon, ed., *op. cit.*, I,
183–87.

[9] This was Isaac's niece, Bagwell's daughter, who married Wormley, one
of the Hemings clan.

[10] In addition to Burwell, who was given $300 "to commence his trade
painter and glazier," John Hemings and Joe Fossett were freed under the
terms of TJ's will. The text of the will is given in the Appendix.

[11] The female slave freed was Harriet, Sally Heming's daughter.

IX

[1] Bacon left Washington about March 9 or 10, 1809: "Gave . . .
E. Bacon for road expences 10.D." (Account Book, March 9, 1809).
In Washington TJ had a number of servants, most of whom were white.

² Bacon's presence at these social functions is doubtful. However, while in Washington he probably did live in the President's house.

³ TJ was interested in the Washington market. He prepared "A Statement of the Vegetable market of Washington, during a period of 8. years, wherein the earliest and latest appearance of each article within the whole 8. years is noted" (*Garden Book,* 639).

⁴ Consult Randall, *op. cit.*, III, 305–6, and Martha Jefferson Randolph to TJ, Feb. 24, 1849, Betts and Bear, eds., *op. cit.*, 384.

⁵ Several errors have crept into Bacon's account of the packing of the books at Monticello and their shipment to Washington. The approximately 6,000 volumes were placed in pine boxes; each box constituted a shelf. The boxes were of three heights, folio, octavo, and duodecimo, but of equal length, and they were attached to each other to form a bank nine feet high. Jefferson oversaw the packing. William D. Johnston, *History of the Library of Congress* (Washington, 1904), I, 65–104, gives the best account of the negotiations for and the transportation of the library to Washington. For the library itself see E. Millicent Sowerby, comp., *Catalogue of the Library of Thomas Jefferson* (Washington, 1952–59), 5 vols.

⁶ The Wythe legacy was received before TJ's sale of his library to Congress in 1815, and the Wythe books were included in the sale.

X

¹ Monroe lived at Ash Lawn a few miles southwest of Monticello.

² Jefferson found the hordes of uninvited guests who flocked to Monticello an aggravating intrusion on his privacy as well as a burden on his finances.

³ Jefferson had endorsed Wilson Cary Nicholas' note for $20,000 and when the latter defaulted payment the burden of meeting this obligation was assumed by the endorser. TJ's finances never recovered from this added burden. Nicholas was buried in the Monticello graveyard.

⁴ Thomas Jefferson Randolph began to assume direction of his grandfather's affairs by 1814, some years before Bacon left Monticello. Probably T. J. Randolph and Bacon did not get along with any degree of cordiality. Pierson says the "letters about Mr. Jefferson" were those published in Randall's *Life of Jefferson.*

⁵ Bacon left Jefferson's service about 1820.

Index

Abraham (slave) , 53
Adams, Abigail (Mrs. John) , 101
Adams, John, 27, 100
Adams, John Quincy, 113
Allen, Hancock, 57
Ampthill, 16
Anderson, Bob (smith) , 7
Anderson, Mat (slave) , 7
Anderson, Richard, 48
Antonine (gardener) , 12
Apples, 100
Arthur (slave) , 17
Artillery, 7
Avery, Mr., 32

Bacon, Capt. Edmund, 27-122 *passim*
Bacon, Mrs. Edmund, 45
Bacon, Fielding, 86
Bacon, Thomas, 86
Bacon, William, 39, 40
Bacon Quarter Branch, 7, 8
Baltimore, Md., 72
Bank of Virginia, 92
Bankhead, Anne Cary (Mrs. Charles L.) , 17, 85, 94
Bankhead, Charles L., 85, 94-96
Barbour, Phil, 95, 96, 112
Barnaby (slave) , 53
Barry, Richard, 55
Bartlet (slave) , 53
Bears, 21
Bedford County, Va., 11
Bedford John (slave) , 53, 63
Belligrini (gardener) , 12

Bellows, 18
Belmont, 20
Belvidere, 20
Belvoir, 26
Ben (slave) , 57
Blenheim, 3, 17
Bolling, John, 18, 22
Bolling, Mary Jefferson (Mrs. John) , 18, 19
Bolling, Ned, *see* John Bolling
Books, 12, 67, 108-110
Botetourt, Norborne Berkeley, Baron de, 5
Bradley, John, 18
Breadmaking, 6
Bringhouse, *see* James Bringhurst
Bringhurst, James, 14, 15
British invasion, 6-10
Brock, John, 21
Brown, Betty (slave) , 54, 59
Buck Island, 21
Burras, Robert, 48
Burras, Thomas, 48
Burwell (slave) , 70, 94, 99, 102
Butler, James, 48
Byrd, Ursula, 5

Caldase, Daniel, 92
Card playing, 21, 72-73
Cardin, William, 92
Carr, Aunt Patsy, *see* Martha Jefferson Carr
Carr, Dabney, 15, 22, 74
Carr, Martha Jefferson (Mrs. Dabney) , 15

Carr, Peter, 15, 74
Carr, Samuel, 15, 74
Carr, Thomas, 48
Carriages, 3, 4, 6, 17, 23, 60, 62, 102, 107
Carroll's farm, 56
Carter, Col. Edward, 3, 17
Cary, Col. Archibald, 3, 15-16, 22
Cary, Nancy, 16
Charles (slave), 53
Charles (white boy), 14
Charlotte County, Va., 29, 35
Charlottesville, Va., 22, 31, 51, 113
Chesterfield County, Va., 18
Chouteau, 42-43
Christmas, 52, 56
Cider, 13, 100
Clark, Gov. William, 34, 41, 42, 43, 44
Clocks, 12-13
Clopton, Rev. Abner W., 29
Clothing, 5, 11, 19-20, 66, 69, 74
Coal, 52
Cocke, Gen. John H., 31, 61
Coles, Edward, 41
Coles, John D., 40
Colle, 12, 22
Cooking, 6
Cooper, Jacob, 48
Copying machine, 12
Corn, 52
Cornwallis, Charles, first Marquis, 10
Coxendale Island, Va., *see* Dutch Gap, Va.
Cows, 63
Craven, John H., 31, 32, 48, 49, 67
Critta (slave), 54, 99
Culpeper Courthouse, Va., 106, 107

Cumberland County, Va., 22
Cups, 14

Daly (Richmond butcher), 7
Dancing, 21, 73
Dangerfield, Miss, 53
Dangerfield, Mrs., 53
Daniel (slave), 10
Daugherty, Joseph, 105
Davy (slave), 47, 49, 55, 63, 104
Davy, Young (slave), 55
Dearborn, Gen. Henry, 59
Deer and deer park, 21
Dewitt (Charlottesville tavern keeper), 22
Didiot (Mazzei's son-in-law), 12
Didiot, Frances, 12
Didiot, Francis, 12
Didiot, Peggy Mazzei, 12
Dinsmore, James, 32, 54, 56, 57, 70, 102
Dogs, 21, 88
Douglas, Rev. William, 5
Drinking, 9, 13, 20, 56, 70
Drums, 7, 10
Dumb-waiter, 12
Durrett, Richard, 82
Dutch Gap, Va., 51

Eda (slave), 104
Edgehill, 16, 22, 89-93
Edwin (slave), 54
Edy (slave), 93
Elk Hill, 17
Elk Island, 17
Eppes, Elizabeth Wayles (Mrs. Francis), 15, 18, 19
Eppes, Francis, 15
Eppes, Francis Wayles, 83
Eppes, Frank, *see* Francis Wayles Eppes
Eppes, Jack, *see* John Wayles Eppes

Eppes, John Wayles, 5, 22, 53, 60, 83

Eppes, Mary Jefferson (Mrs. John Wayles), 5, 15, 17, 22, 83, 100, 101

Fanny (slave), 55, 104
Fauble, Mr. (French musician), 13
Fences, 21, 52, 55, 56, 87
Fennel (slave), 93
Firewood, 55, 66, 80, 81
Fires and fire-fighting, 22
Fleming, Col. William, 3
Flogging, 16, 97, 98
Flour, 79; *see also* Shadwell mill
Fosset, Joe (slave), 54, 102
Francis (gardener), 12
Franklin rod, 3
Fredericksburg, Va., 13
Freeman, John H., 54
French people, 13

Gardens, 12, 18, 46, 47, 49, 50, 52, 87, 88
Garnett, James, 40
Gates, 15
George (Isaac's father, slave), 3, 8, 10, 21
Georgetown, D.C., 13, 47
German soldiers, 20
Giles, William B., 17
Gilmer, Walker, 87
Ginger cakes, 6
Giovanni (Williamsburg tailor), 5
Goats, 22
Goochland County, Va., 3
Goode, Col. Francis, 20
Gordon, Nat, 13
Gordon, William F., 87, 95, 96, 112

Governor's House (Richmond), 8-9
Grady (nailery overseer), 97, 98
Graves, Capt. John, 62, 74
Guns, 17

Harvie, Col. John (Jack), 20
Harvie, Mrs. John, 20
Hemings, Betty (slave), 4, 6, 54, 99
Hemings, Harriet (slave), 4
Hemings, James (Jim, slave), 4, 6, 13, 15
Hemings, John (slave), 19, 54, 101, 102, 109
Hemings, Madison (slave), 4
Hemings, Martin (slave), 4, 6
Hemings, Mary (slave), 4, 6, 7, 8, 10
Hemings, Peter (slave), 54
Hemings, Robert (Bob, slave), 4, 6, 13, 15
Hemings, Sally (slave), 4, 54, 99, 100, 101
Hemings family, *see* Genealogical Table B, opp. p. 24
Henrico Courthouse, Va., 22
Henry, Patrick, 11
Herring, 23
Higginbotham, David, 54, 56
Hogs, 47, 48, 59, 66, 115
Horse racing, 20, 35-36
Horses, 5, 8, 11, 13-14, 20, 35-36, 41, 60-62, 69, 73-74, 89, 106
Hubbard, Jame (Jim; slave), 53, 63, 97-98
Hubbard, Phill (slave), 53, 63
Hunting, 17-18, 21
Hylton, Daniel, 9

Imboden, Mr., 61
Indian remains, 22
Iris (slave), 92

Ironing, 8
Isaac (slave), 3-24 *passim* and Genealogical Table A, opp. p. 24
Isaacs, Davy, 32, 61
Isaac's wife, 23
Isbel's Davy (slave), 53
Italians, 12, 23

Jackson, Andrew, 113
Jamestown, Va., 22
Jamison, Dr., 113
Jefferson, Anna Scott, *see* Anna Scott Marks
Jefferson, George, 54
Jefferson, Lucy, 19
Jefferson, Martha (TJ's daughter), *see* Martha Jefferson Randolph
Jefferson, Martha Wayles (Mrs. Thomas), 3-5, 99, 100
Jefferson, Mary (Pol, Polly, Maria, TJ's daughter), *see* Mary Jefferson Eppes
Jefferson, Mary (TJ's sister), *see* Mary Jefferson Bolling
Jefferson, Nancy, *see* Anna Scott Marks
Jefferson, Patsy, *see* Martha Wayles Jefferson; Martha Jefferson Carr; Martha Jefferson Randolph
Jefferson, Polly, *see* Mary Jefferson Bolling; Mary Jefferson Eppes
Jefferson, Randolph (TJ's brother), 22
Jefferson, Thomas ("Old Master"), 3-122 *passim*
Jerry (slave), 53, 62, 68
Jim (slave), 51
Joe (slave), 10
John (slave), 5, 6, 11, **52, 53**

Johnson, Absalom, 40
Johnson, Chapman, 31, 33, 112
Jovanini (gardener), 12
Julien (TJ's French cook), 104
Jupiter (slave), 5, 6, 10

Kelly, John, 49
Kentucky, 78
Keys and locks, 18

Lafayette, Marquis de, 19
Lego (one of TJ's farms), 51
Lemaire, Etienne, 105
Lewis (slave), 53
Lewis, Nicholas, 31, 32
Lilly, Gabriel, 54
Little York, *see* Yorktown
London, 4
Looming, 19
Louisa County, Va., 62

Maddox, William, 65
Madison, James, 31, 58, 59, 62, 102, 103, 111-113
Madzay, *see* Philip Mazzei
Maine, Thomas, 47, 49, 106
Manchester, Va., 7
Maria (slave), 92
Marks, Anna Scott (Mrs. Hastings), 22
Marks, Hastings, 22
Marr, James, 81
Marsdell, Mr., *see* James Marsden
Marsden, James, 7
Martin (slave), 53
Massey, Mr., 77
Mazzei, Philip, 12, 23
Merriwether, Mr., 56
Mill, *see* Shadwell mill
Millbrook, 22
Milton, 16, 51, 80
Minor, Peter, 66

Missouri, 40, 42, 43
Modena (gardener), 12
Molasses, 23
Molly (slave), 10
Molly (John Page's slave), 11
Monroe, James, 31, 33, 37, 69, 111-113
Mont Blanco (Mount Black), 22
Monticello, 3-122 *passim*
Montpelier, 58
Moses (slave), 53
Moldboard, 73
Mules, 55, 65, 66, 77, 78
Music, 4, 13, 22

Nails and nailery, 16, 23, 53, 56, 69, 97-98, 111-112
Nance (slave), 52, 54, 99
Nancy, *see* Anna Scott Marks
Neilson, John, 3, 55
Nelson, Mr., *see* John Neilson
Nelson, Hugh, 78
Nicholas, Jane Hollins, 17, 85
Nicholas, Wilson Cary, 85, 115
North Carolina, University, 29

Oglesby (Charlottesville teacher), 87
Orr (Ore), Billy, 3, 4, 20

Page, Gov. John, 11
Page, Mann, 51
Pantops (one of TJ's farms), 51
Partridges, 17, 18
Patsy, *see* Martha Jefferson Carr; Martha Jefferson Randolph; Martha Wayles Jefferson
Perry, John M., 31, 32, 50, 56
Petersburg, Va., 4, 7, 18
Peyton, John, 48, 66, 67
Philadelphia, 13-16

Piragua, 10
Ploughing, 52
Pocahontas, Va., 23
Polygraph, 12
Pompey (horse trainer), 20
Poplar Forest (TJ's farm in Bedford Co.), 11, 56, 62, 67, 68, 114
Powder magazine, 9
Powhatan house, 6
President's House, 104, 105

Rabbits, 20, 21, 50
Randolph, Anne Cary, *see* Anne Cary Bankhead
Randolph, Benjamin Franklin, 17, 85
Randolph, Cornelia Jefferson, 17, 85, 119
Randolph, Ellen Wayles, 85, 89, 109
Randolph, George Wythe, 85
Randolph, James Madison, 17, 85
Randolph, John, of Roanoke, 29, 35-36, 90
Randolph, Martha Jefferson (Mrs. Thomas Mann, Jr.), 3, 5, 15, 16, 54, 83-86, 114
Randolph, Meriwether Lewis, 85
Randolph, Septimia Anne, 85
Randolph, Thomas Jefferson, 11, 17, 80, 85, 87, 94, 103, 115-116
Randolph, Thomas Mann, Sr., 11, 16
Randolph, Thomas Mann, Jr., 3, 16, 22, 52, 53, 67, 71, 85, 89-94
Randolph, Virginia Jefferson, 85, 109
Randolph family, 90
Rapin, Joseph, 13, 15, 20
Ratiff, Joseph, *see* Joseph Rapin

Redhazel, General, *see* Baron de Riedesel
Religion, 109, 110
Richmond, Va., 6, 7, 8, 11, 20, 67, 89, 115
Riedesel, Baron de, 12, 22
Rives, William Cabell, 8, 87-89
Roach, Capt. C. W., 28-30
Rogers, Mr., 56
Rogers, John, 48
Rum, 9, 13

St. Louis, Mo., 42–45
School, at Monticello, 18
Servants, 5, 15, 52, 54, 97-99, 101, 104, 105
Shadwell (one of TJ's farms), 51
Shadwell mill, 47, 52, 53, 56, 64-68, 71-72, 79, 88
Sheep, 22, 47, 58-59, 73
Shew, Mr., 23
Shoemaker, Jonathan?, 64, 65
Silver, 8, 11
Simcoe, Col. J. G., 8
Skelton, Bathurst, 3
Skelton, Martha Wayles (Mrs. Bathurst), *see* Martha Wayles Jefferson
Skipper, Mrs., *see* Mrs. Fulwar Skipwith
Skipwith, Mrs. Fulwar, 18
Skipwith, William, 22
Slaves: 23, 48, 53-54, 66, 69, 72-73, 91-93, 97-98, 102-103, 104
South Octagon, 18
Southall, Vaul W., 87, 88, 112
Spotswood, Dandridge, 23
Squirrels, 17
Stewart, William, 48, 54, 69, 70, 102
Strauss, Dr. George F., 4
Sukey (slave), 10

Tailors, 5
Temple, Col. Robert, 16
Terril, Robert, 48
Thorns, 49, 55, 65
Threshing machine, 22
Tin business, 14-15, 16
Tobacco, 72
Trees, 49, 50, 55, 56
Trigg County, Ky., 28
Tuckahoe, 9
"Tuckahoe Tom," *see* Thomas Mann Randolph, Sr.
Tufton (one of TJ's farms), 51

United States Bank, 69, 92
Ursula (Usley or Usler, Isaac's mother), 3, 8, 10, 54, 99, 101

Varina, 22
Virginia, University of, 81, 34, 76, 87, 102

Wagons, 4, 10, 62
Walker, Col., 78
Walker, Frank, 78
Walker, John, 12
Walker, Dr. Thomas, 12
Wallers, James O., 92
Wallis, *see* Charles Cornwallis, first Marquis
Warm Springs, Va., 40
Washing, 8
Washington, George, 11, 14, 18, 19
Washington, D.C., 99, 104, 105
Washington Tavern, 9
Watson, Billy, 20
Watson, Davy, 3, 4, 20
Wayles, Francis, 22
Wells, Thomas, 96
Westham, 9
Whiskey, 56
Wildcats, 21

Wiley, Billy, 6
Wiley, Mrs. Billy, 6
William and Mary College, 5
Williamsburg, Va., 4, 5, 6, 7
Willis' Mountain, 19
Wine, 9, 13

Winny (slave), 96
Wintopoke, 15
Wolves, 21
Wormley (slave), 10, 50, 63, 65
Wythe, George, 1, 110

Yorktown, Va., 10, 11